Tchaikovsky's Complete Song Texts

Russian texts of the complete songs of

Peter Ilyich Tchaikovsky

with phonetic transcriptions,

literal and idiomatic English translations

by

Laurence R. Richter

TCHAIKOVSKY'S COMPLETE SONG TEXTS

by Laurence R. Richter

ISBN 1-878617-29-X

LEYERLE PUBLICATIONS
Executive Offices
28 Stanley Street
Mt. Morris, New York 14510

This book can be ordered directly from

LEYERLE PUBLICATIONS

Box 384
Geneseo, New York 14454

Table of Contents

Key to Russian Phonetic Transcription for Singers

VOWELS

The vowels of Russian are pronounced essentially like Italian vowels, with the exception of [y]. The vowel [y] is an [i] pronounced mid-high and central, rather than high and front. It is always preceded by a hard consonant. It is not in any way diphthongal. It is just as much pure vowel as [i], but is pronounced lower and farther back. (Russians sometimes pronounce this vowel with a slight rounding assimilation ([^{w}y]), but only after labials (b,p,v,f, m). Foreigners should avoid doing so, because of their tendency to over-do and over-extend this optional, slight assimilation.)

Russian has both open [ɛ] (French è) and close [e] (French é).

Russian schwa, [ə], common in speech, has a restricted distribution in singing. It equates to English about, lemon, circus, sofa, element, etc.

CONSONANTS

Nearly all Russian consonants can occur either as palatalized (soft) or unpalatalized (hard). Palatalization is symbolized in transcription by a little hook on the consonant letter: [b̡], [p̡], [d̡], [t̡], etc.

Palatalization is a salient characteristic of Russian phonology. It is the releasing of a consonant in the palate, accomplished by arching the tongue up into the palate and "squeezing" the consonant sound down from above. The place of consonantal palatalization is precisely where the vowel [i] is located in the oral cavity. Palatalization is therefore also characterized as "i-coloring" of the consonant.

Another characteristic of palatalized stops (b,d,g,p,t,k) is that they take on a fricative quality, a kind of "slipperiness," an extendibility that stops otherwise lack.

Foreigners should avoid substituting consonant + sibilant release for palatalized consonants: [ts] instead of [t̡], [dz] instead of [d̡], etc. Even worse is the substitution of hard consonant + English y for palatalized consonants: d+ya instead of [d̡a], l+yu instead of [l̡u], b+yo instead of [b̡o], etc. Such mispronunciations are often the direct result of working from a transliteration rather than a transcription, and strike the Russian ear as very un-Russian and very ugly.

Some of the symbols used differ from the usual IPA representations. They are instead the symbols familiar to all scholars dealing with Slavic languages. For a variety of reasons, the author considers them more practical for use here than their IPA equivalents. Note the following:

[ž] English azure, pleasure. Always hard.
[š] English sure, **sh**ip. Always hard.
[c] English **ts**e**ts**e. German zu. Always hard.
[ž̡ž̡] Long, soft [ž].
[š̡š̡] Long, soft [š].
[č̡] English **ch**ur**ch**. Always soft.

[j] German **j**a, **j**ung.

[x] German Ba**ch**.

[ɣ] Voiced [x], or [g] rendered as a fricative. Spanish a**g**ua. This sound occurs only when [x] is followed by a voiced consonant. (See ASSIMILATIONS below.)

[dz] Voiced [c]. This sound occurs only when [c] is followed by a voiced consonant. (See ASSIMILATIONS below.)

[ḑž̧] English **judg**e. This sound occurs only when [ç̌] is followed by a voiced consonant. (See ASSIMILATIONS below.)

Hard consonants in general are pronounced much like their English counterparts, except that voiced consonants get heavier voicing than in English, and there is no aspiration of stops.

Russian hard [l] merits special mention, since it is much harder than even English final "dark" l and affords, by its mispronunciation, one of the most common giveaways of a non-Russian singer. Hard [l] is pronounced with the tongue in the same contour as in English r: **earn, earth**, etc. A good exercise for practicing Russian hard l is to say English **grr**, then hold everything in place except the tip of the tongue, which moves forward only far enough to make dental contact, and say **girl** with the l in the throat, as if gargling with it, and hold onto it as long as breath allows. That's Russian hard [l]; and the substitution of a "continental" l for it sounds comically wrong to the Russian ear.

When a consonant in transcription is followed by the diacritic ‾ (d‾, ŗ‾, etc.), this indicates that the consonant in this environment is not released. (The first t is English **nitrate** is released; the first t in English **night rate** is not.)

N.B. The author is aware that the conventional way of indicating length in phonetic transcriptions is the use of the symbol : . But experience has also made him aware that singers tend to ignore the symbol : after another symbol. Length is much more likely to be realized when the consonant symbol is doubled. Therefore the symbolizations [ž̧ž̧] and [ş̌ş̌] indicate these consonants' *length*, and not doubling. There is no danger of confusing these symbols with the actual doubling of the consonants [ž] and [š], since these sounds are always hard and would lack the palatalization markers.

ASSIMILATIONS

Voiced:	[b]	[d]	[g]	[v]	[z]	[ž]	[ž̧ž̧]	([dz])	([ḑž̧])	([ɣ])
Voiceless:	[p]	[t]	[k]	[f]	[s]	[š]	[ş̌ş̌]	[c]	[ç̌]	[x]

As in German, final Russian consonants can be only voiceless. Words ending in a voiced consonant are therefore pronounced with the final consonant devoiced: [p] for graphic **b**, [t] for graphic **d**, [k] for graphic **g**, and so forth. Thus, раб [rɑp], род [rot], друг [druk], etc.

However, devoicing of consonants does not occur if it violates an even stronger phonological principle of Russian, namely, *consonant assimilation*. When two or more consonants are pronounced together without pause in Russian -- whether within the same syllable, over syllable boundaries, or even over word boundaries -- they must all be voiced, or they must all be voiceless. Thus, not only must one sing водка as [vótka] and просьба as [prózʲba], but also: раб дул [rab‿dul], род был [rod‿byl], друг жал [drug‿žal], etc. Such non-devoicings of final consonants are marked in the transcription with a ligature: ‿ . The singer should devoice the consonant to the left of the ligature if he decides to break the phrase at this point.

The same ligature is used to indicate vocalic assimilations.

Close [e] occurs in Russian only **before** a palatalized consonant or a front vowel, [i] or [e]. Elsewhere only open [ɛ] occurs. Consequently, if word-final **-e** is followed without pause by a word beginning with a palatalized consonant or a front vowel, it is transcribed as [e] and is followed by a ligature: ‿. The singer who opts to break here, however, must sing the **-e** as [ɛ].

Similarly, the vowel [y] occurs only **after** an unpalatalized, or hard, consonant (explaining why this sound could never be initial). This positional variant of /i/ is therefore the only vowel realizable after a hard consonant, whether reflected in the spelling or not. A hard consonant cannot be followed by [i]; and a soft consonant cannot be followed by [y]. Thus, вот и он [vot‿y on]; дал им [dal‿ym]; к Ире [k‿yrʲɛ]; etc. Should a break be introduced at the point of the ligature, the vowel after the break would then be pronounced [i].

N.B. The symbol # has been used in the literal translations to indicate that a Russian word does not translate. It therefore has no correspondence in the English translation.

П. Чайковский

1. Мой гений, мой ангел, мой друг... 'My genius, my angel, my friend...'

(A. Fet) (Late 1850's)

Не здесь ли ты лёгкою тенью, Мой гений, мой ангел, мой друг,
[n̦e‿z̦d̦éș l̦i ty l̦óxkɑju țén̦ju mój g̦én̦ij mój ɑ́ng̦ɛl mój drúk]
not here # you like-light shadow my genius my angel my friend
Are you not here, like a light shadow, my genius, my angel, my friend,

Беседуешь тихо со мною И тихо летаешь вокруг?
[b̦eșéduješ țíxɑ sɑmnóju i țíxɑ lɛtájɛš vɑkrúk]
[you-converse quietly with-me and quietly fly about
Conversing quietly with me and fluttering quietly about?

И робким даришь вдохновеньем, И сладкий врачуешь недуг,
[i rópķim dɑr̦íž‿vdɑxnɑv̦én̦jɛm i slɑ́tkəj vrɑč̦újɛš n̦ɛdúk]
and shy you-grant inspiration and sweet you-heal ailment
And granting me shy inspiration and healing my sweet ailment,

И тихим даришь сновиденьем Мой гений, мой ангел, мой друг...
[i țíx̦im dɑr̦íš snɑv̦id̦én̦jɛm mój g̦én̦ij mój ɑ́ng̦ɛl mój drúk]
and quiet you-grant dream my genius my angel my friend
And granting me quiet dreams, my genius, my angel, my friend.

2. Песнь Земфиры 'Zemfira's Song'

(A. Pushkin) (Early 1860's)

Старый муж, грозный муж, режь меня, Старый муж, грозный муж, жги меня.
[stáryj múš gróznyj múš r̦éš m̦en̦ɑ́ stáryj múš gróznyj múš žg̦í m̦en̦ɑ́]
old husband terrible husband cut me old husband terrible husband burn me
My old husband, threatening husband, stab me! My old husband, threatening husband, burn me!

Я тверда, не боюсь ни огня, ни меча. Режь меня, жги меня!
[ja tv̦ɛrdɑ́ n̦ɛbajúș n̦i ɑgn̦ɑ́ n̦i m̦eč̦ɑ́ r̦éš m̦en̦ɑ́ žg̦í m̦en̦ɑ́]
I [am] hard I- not-fear neither flame nor sword cut me burn me
I am hard, and I fear neither flame now sword. Stab me, burn me!

Ненавижу тебя, презираю тебя; Я другого люблю, умираю любя.
[ņεnaγížu ţeþá pŗeziráju ţeþá ja drugóva ļuþļú uḿiráju ļuþá]
I-hate you [I] despise you. I another I-love I- die loving [him]
I hate you, I despise you. I love another, and I will die loving him.

АЛЕКО: Молчи. Мне пенье надоело, Я диких песен не люблю.
(Aleko) [malçí mņe‿péņjε nadajéla ja díķix pésεn ņeļuþļú]
be-still to-me singing has-become-annoying I wild songs not-like
Be still. I'm fed up with your singing. I don't like wild songs.

ЗЕМФИРА: Не любишь? Мне какое дело? Я песню для себя пою.
(Zemfira) [ņeļúþiš mņέ kakóje‿déla ja péşņu dļaşeþá pajú
you- not-like to-me what matter I song for-self sing
You don't like it? What do I care? I am singing for myself.

Он свежее весны, жарче летнего дня;
[ón şγεžéje‿γεsný žárçe‿ļétņεva dņá]
he [is] fresher [than]-spring hotter [than]-summer day
He is fresher than spring, hotter than a summer day.

Как он молод и смел! Как он любит меня!
[kák ón mólat‿y şmέl kákón ļúþit meņá]
how he young and bold [is] how he loves me
How young and bold he is! How he loves me!

АЛЕКО: Земфира!
(Aleko) [zεmfíra]
Zemfira!

ЗЕМФИРА: Ты сердиться волен, Я песню про тебя пою.
(Zemfira) [ty şεrdítca vóļεn já péşņu praţeþá pajú]
you to-become-angry [are] free I song about-you sing
Become as angry as you like. I am singing about you.

3. Не верь, мой друг... 'Believe it not, my friend...' Соч. 6, № 1
(A.K. Tolstoy) (1869)

Не верь, мой друг, не верь, когда в порыве горя
[ņeγéŗ mój drúk ņeγéŗ kagdá fparýγε góŗa]
not believe my friend not believe when in-burst of-woe
Do not believe me, my friend, do not believe me, when, in a fit of despair,

Я говорю, что разлюбил тебя, --в отлива час не верь,
[ja gavaŗú što razļub̧il ţeb̧á vatļíva ç̌ás ņev̧éŗ]
I say that [I]-have-stopped-loving you at-of-low-tide hour not-believe
I say that I no longer love you. Do not believe, at the hour of low-tide,

Не верь измене моря, оно к земле воротится любя.
[ņev̧éŗ izm̧éņɛ móŗa anó gz̧em̧ļɛ́ varóţitca ļub̧á]
not-believe betrayal of-sea it to-land will-return loving
Do not believe the betrayal of the sea, it will return lovingly to the land.

Уж я тоскую, прежней страсти полный, Свою свободу вновь тебе отдам --
[úž ja taskúju p̧ŗɛ́žņej strás̨ţi pólnyj svajú svabódu vnóf̧ ţeb̧ɛ́ addám]
I grieve of-former passion full my freedom anew to-you [I]- will-give
I am anguished, filled with a former passion. I will again yield to you my freedom--

И уж бегут обратно с шумом волны Издалека к любимым берегам.
[i už‿b̧egút abrátna ššúmam vólny izdaļɛká kļub̧ímym b̧eŗɛgám]
and already they-run back with-noise waves from-afar to-beloved shores
And now the waves come rushing back noisily, from afar, to the beloved shores.

4. Ни слова, о друг мой... 'Not a word, oh my friend...' Соч. 6, № 2
(A. Pleshcheev, after Hartmann) (1869)

Ни слова, о друг мой, ни вздоха... Мы будем с тобой молчаливы...
[ņi slóva o drúk mój ņi vzdóxa my búḑɛm stabój malç̌aļívy]
not word oh friend my not sigh we will-be with-you silent
Not a word, my friend, not a sigh... We will remain silent...

Ведь молча над камнем, над камнем могильным Склоняются грустные ивы...
[v̧eţ mólç̌a natkámņɛm natkámņɛm maģíļnymsklaņájutca grúsnyjɛ ívy]
indeed silently over-stone over-stone of-tomb are-leaning mournful willows
Indeed, over the tombstone silently lean mournful willows.

И только, склонившись, читают, Как я в твоём сердце усталом,
[i tóļka sklaņífšys̨ ç̌itájut kak já ftvajóm s̨értcɛ ustálam]
and only having-leaned-down read as I in-your heart weary
And, leaning down, they read, as I read in your weary heart,

Что были дни ясного счастья, Что этого счастья не стало!
[što býļi dņí jásnava ş̧ş̧áşţja što étava ş̧ş̧áşţja ņɛstála]
thatwere days of-bright happines thatthis happiness did-not-last
That there were days of calm happiness, that this happiness is no more.

5. И больно, и сладко... 'Both painful and sweet...' Соч. 6, № 3
(E. Rostopchina) (1869)

И больно, и сладко, когда при начале любви
[i bóļna i slátka kagdá pŗinaçáļe‿ļubví]
bothpainful andsweet when at-beginning of-love
It is both painful and sweet when, at love's start,

То сердце забьётся украдкой, то в жилах течёт лихорадка,
[to şértcɛ zaþjótca ukrátkəj to vžýlax ţeçót ļixarátka]
firstheart will-beat furtively then in-veins flows fever
First the heart beats furtively, then a fever rages through the veins.

И больно, и сладко; то жар запылает в крови... И больно и сладко!
[i bóļna i slátka to žár zapylájɛt fkraví i boļna i slátka]
bothpainful and sweet then blaze flares-up in-blood both painful andsweet
It is both painful and sweet. Then a blaze flares up in the blood-- both painful and sweet!

Пробьёт час свиданья,-- потупя предательский взор,
[praþjót çás şvidáņja patúpa pŗɛdáţeļskəj vzór]
will-sound hour of-rendezvous lowering betraying gaze
The hour of encounter sounds--lowering the give-away gaze,

В волненьи, в томленьи незнанья боишься,
[vvalņéņji ftamļéņji ņɛznáņja baíšsa]
in-agitation in-stupor of-not-knowing [you] fear
In agitation and suspense, you are afraid,

Желаешь признанья,-- и в муку свиданье!
[žɛlájɛš pŗiznáņja i vmúku şvidáņjɛ]
[you] desire admission and to-torment meeting
You want to declare your love--but the meeting is torture.

Начнёшь и прервёшь разговор...
[načņóš i pŗɛŗyóš razgavór
[you] will-begin and will-cut-off conversation
Your conversation starts and stops...

И в муку свиданье! Не вымолвишь слова...
[i vmúku şyidáŋjɛ ŋɛvýmalyiš slóva]
and to-torment rendezvous [you]-will-not-utter word
And the rendezvous is torture. You can't get a word out,

Немеешь, робеешь, дрожишь;
[ŋeméjɛš raḅéjɛš dražýš]
[you] grow-dumb become-shy tremble
You become speechless, shy, you tremble.

Душа, проклиная оковы, вся в речи излиться готова...
[dušá prakļinája akóvy fşá vŗéçi izļítca gatóva]
[your] soul cursing [its] fetters [is] all in-speech to-pour-out ready
Your soul, cursing its fetters, is all ready to burst into speech.

Нет силы, нет слова, и только глядишь и молчишь!
[ŋét şíly ŋét slóva i tóļka g ļaḑíš i malçíš]
is-not strength is-not word and only [you] gaze and are-silent
You are powerless, speechless, and can only stare silently.

И сладко, и больно... И трепет безумный затих;
[i slátka i bóļna i ţŗépɛd‿ḅɛzúmnyj zaţíx]
both sweet and painful and trembling mad has-grown-quiet
It is both sweet and painful. And later the mad trepidation passes

И сердцу легко и раздольно... Слова полились бы так вольно,
[i şértcu ļɛxkó i razdóļna slavá paļiļíz‿by tak vóļna]
and to-heart easy and carefree words pour-forth would so freely
And your heart becomes light and free. Words could gush forth so freely...

И сладко, и больно, Но слушать уж некому их.
[i slátka i bóļna no slúšaţ už ŋékamu ix]
both sweet and painful but to-listen already no-one to-them
It is both sweet and painful, but now there is no one to hear them.

6. Слеза дрожит... 'A tear trembles...'

Соч. 6, № 4

(A.K. Tolstoy)

(1869)

Слеза дрожит в твоём ревнивом взоре... О, не грусти, ты всё мне дорога!
[şļɛzá dražýt ftvajóm ŗɛvņívam vzóŗɛ o ņɛgruşţí ty fşo mņɛ daragá]
tear trembles in-your jealous gaze oh not-grieve you still to-me dear
A tear trembes in your jealous gaze. Oh, do not grieve, you are still dear to me.

Но я любить могу лишь на просторе, Мою любовь, широкую, как море,
[no já ļuþíţ magú ļiš naprastóŗɛ majú ļubóf šyrókuju kak móŗɛ]
but I to-love can only in-open-space my love broad as sea
But my love must have free range. My love, as broad as the sea,

Вместить не могут, нет! вместить не могут Жизни берега.
[vmeşţíţ ņɛmógut ņét vmeşţíţ ņɛmógut žýzņi þeŗɛgá]
to-fit-in not-they-can no to-fit-in not-they-can [within] of-life shores
Cannot be contained, no, cannot be contained by life's shores.

О, не грусти, мой друг, земное минет горе, Пожди ещё, неволя недолга.
[o ņɛgruşţí mój drúk ȥɛmnóje‿míņɛd‿góŗɛ paždí jeşşó ņɛvóļa ņɛdalgá]
oh not-grieve my friend earthly will-pass woe wait yet captivity not-long
Oh do not grieve, my friend, earth's woes will pass. Wait a bit, our bondage is not forever.

В одну любовь мы все сольёмся вскоре, В одну любовь, широкую, как море,
[vadnú ļubóf my fşé saļjómsa fskóŗɛ vadnú ļubóf šyrókuju kak móŗɛ]
into-one love we all will-merge soon into-one love broad as sea
Soon we shall all be joined in one love, in one love as broad as the sea

Что не вместят, нет! что не вместят Земные берега!
[štó ņeymeşţát ņét štó ņeymeşţát ȥɛmnýje‿þeŗɛgá]
which not-they- will-fit no which not-they-will-fit [within] earthly shores
Which will not be contained, no, not be contained by Earth's shores.

7. Отчего?... 'Why?...'

Соч. 6, № 5

(L. Mey, after Heine)

(1869)

Отчего побледнела весной Пышноцветная роза сама?
[atçɛvó paþļɛdņéla ɣɛsnój pyšnacɣétnaja róza samá]
why has-grown-pale in-spring luxuriantly-flowered rose itself
Why, in springtime, has the rose in full bloom grown pale?

Отчего под зелёной травой Голубая фиалка нема?
[atç̌εvó padz̧eļónəj travój galubája f̧iálka ņεmá]
why under-green grass blue violet mute
Why has the blue violet among the blades of green grass grown mute?

Отчего так печально звучит Песня птички, несясь в небеса?
[atç̌εvó tak p̧eç̌áļna zvuç̌ít p̧éşņa p̧ţíç̌ķi ņeşáş vņeb̧εsá]
why so sad sounds song of-bird flying to-skies
Why does the song of the bird, heaven bound, sound so sad?

Отчего над лугами висит Погребальным покровом роса?
[atç̌εvó nadlugám̧i v̧işit pag̨ŗεbáļnym pakróvam rasá]
why above-meadows hangs like-funeral pall dew
Why does the dew hang like a funeral pall over the meadows?

Отчего в небе солнце с утра Холодно и темно, как зимой?
[atç̌εvó vņéb̧ε sóncε sutrá xaladnó i ţεmnó kag‿z̧imój]
why in-sky sun in-morning cold and dark as in-winter
Why does the morning sun seem as cold and dark as in winter?

Отчего и земля вся сыра И угрюмей могилы самой?
[atç̌εvó i z̧em̧ļá f̧şá syrá i ugŗúm̧ej mag̨íly samój]
why and earth all moist and gloomier than-tomb itself
Why is the whole Earth dank and gloomier than the tomb itself?

Отчего я и сам всё грустней И болезненней день ото дня?
[atç̌εvó ja i sám f̧şó gruşņéj i baļéz̧ņeņņej ḑéņ ataḑņá]
why I too self more-and-more mournful and more-sickly day to-day
Why do I myself also grow more mournful and sickly day after day?

Отчего, о, скажи мне скорей, Ты, покинув, забыла меня?
[atç̌εvó o skažý mņέ skaŗéj ty pak̨ínuf zabýla m̧eņá]
why oh tell me quickly you having-left [me] have-forgotten me
Why, oh tell me, please, have you abandoned and forgotten me?

8. Нет, только тот, кто знал... 'None but the lonely heart...' Соч. 6, № 6
(L. Mey, after Goethe) (1869)

Нет, только тот, кто знал свиданья жажду,
[ṇ̑ɛ́t tóḷka tót któ znál ṣṿidáṇja žáždu]
no only he who has-known of-meeting thirst
No, only he who has known the longing again to see his beloved

Поймёт, как я страдал и как я стражду.
[pajṃót kak já stradál i kák ja stráždu]
will-understand how I suffered and how I am-suffering
Can understand how I have suffered and I suffer still.

Гляжу я в даль... нет сил, тускнеет око...
[gḷažú ja vdáḷ ṇét ṣíl tuskṇéjɛt óka]
gaze I in-distance is-not strength grows-dim eye
I gaze into the distance... I am powerless, my eyes dim.

Ах, кто меня любил и знал,-- далёко!
[áx któ ṃeṇá ḷuḅil‿y znál daḷóka]
ah who me loved and knew far-away
Ah, the one who knew and loved me best is far away.

Ах, только тот, кто знал свиданья жажду,
[áx tóḷka tót któ znál ṣṿidáṇja žáždu]
no only he who has-known of-meeting thirst
No, only he who has known the longing again to see his beloved

Поймёт,как я страдал и как я стражду.
[pajṃót kak já stradál i kák ja stráždu]
will-understand how I suffered and how I am-suffering
Can understand how I have suffered and I suffer still.

Вся грудь горит... Кто знал свиданья жажду,
[f̣ṣá grúḍ‿gaṛít któ znál ṣṿidáṇja žáždu]
whole breast burns who has-known of-meeting thirst
My heart is ablaze... He who has known the longing again to see his beloved

Поймёт, как я страдал и как я стражду.
[pajṃót kak já stradál i kák ja stráždu]
will-understand how I suffered and how I am-suffering
Can understand how I have suffered and I suffer still.

9. Забыть так скоро... 'So soon forgotten...'

(A. Apukhtin) (1870)

Забыть так скоро, Боже мой, Всё счастье жизни прожитой!
[zabýţ¯ ták skóra bóžɛ mój f̧şó ş̌ş̌áşţjɛ žýz̧ņi pražytój]
to-forget so soon God my all happiness of-life past
So soon forgotten, my God! All the happiness of our shared life.

Все наши встречи, разговоры Забыть так скоро, забыть так скоро!
[f̧şɛ́ nášy f̧şţŗéç̌i razgavóry zabýţ¯ ták skóra zabýţ¯ ták skóra]
all our meetings conversations to-forget so soon to-forget so soon
All our times together, talks... So soon forgotten, so soon forgotten!

Забыть волненья первых дней, Свиданья час в тени ветвей!
[zabýţ valņéņja p̧ɛ́rvyɣ‿ḑņéj şv̧idáņja ç̌ás fţeņí v̧eţv̧éj]
to-forget excitements of-first days of-meeting hour in-shade of-branches
To forget the intensity of those first days, the hour or meeting under the shady branches.

Очей немые разговоры Забыть так скоро, забыть так скоро!
[aç̌éj ņɛmýjɛ razgavóry zabýţ¯ ták skóra zabýţ¯ ták skóra]
of-eyes mute conversations to-forgetso soon to-forget so soon
The wordless conversations of our eyes, so soon forgotten, so soon forgotten!

Забыть, как полная луна На нас глядела из окна,
[zabýţ kak pólnaja luná nanáz‿ģļaḑɛ́la izakná]
to-forget how full moon on-us gazed through-window
To forget how the full moon gazed upon us through the window,

Как колыхалась тихо штора... Забыть любовь, забыть мечты,
[kak kalyxálaş ţíxa štóra zabýţ ļubóf̧ zabýţ m̧eç̌tý]
how rustled quietly drape to-forgetlove to-forget dreams
How the drape rustled quietly. To forget our love, to forget our dreams,

Забыть те клятвы, помнишь ты, В ночную пасмурную пору?
[zabýţ¯ ţe‿ķļátvy pómņiš ty vnaç̌núju pásmurnuju póru]
to-forget those oaths remember you in-nocturnal bleak time
To forget our pledges, remember? in that bleak night?

Забыть так скоро, Боже мой!
[zabýţ¯ ták skóra bóžɛ mój]
to-forget so soon God my
So soon forgotten! My God!

10. Колыбельная песня*　'Lullabye'　　Соч. 16, № 1
(A. Maikov)　　(1872)

Спи, дитя моё, спи, усни!　Спи, усни!　Сладкий сон к себе мани.
[s̡p̡í d̡it̡ɑ́ mɑjó s̡p̡í us̡n̡í　s̡p̡í us̡n̡í　slɑ́tkəj són ks̡eb̡ɛ́　mɑn̡í]
sleep child my　sleep fall-asleep sleep fall-asleep sweet　sleep to-yourself entice
Sleep, my child, sleep, fall asleep.　Let sweet dreams overtake you.

В няньки я тебе взяла　Ветер, солнце и орла.
[vn̡ɑ́n̡k̡i jɑ t̡eb̡é‿v̡z̡ɑlɑ́　v̡ét̡ɛr sónce‿i　ɑrlɑ́]
as-nannies I　for-you have-taken wind　sun　and eagle
As your nannies I have summoned the wind, the sun, and the eagle.

Улетел орёл домой;　Солнце скрылось под водой;
[ul̡et̡ɛ́l　ɑr̡ól dɑmój sóncɛ skrýlɑs̡ pɑdvɑdój]
flew-away eagle home　sun　hid　under- water
The eagle flew away home, the sun sank beneath the water;

Ветер после трёх ночей　Мчится к матери своей.
[v̡ét̡ɛr pos̡l̡et̡r̡óx nɑč̡éj　mč̡ítcɑ　kmɑ́t̡er̡i svɑjéj]
wind　after-three　nights　rushes　to-mother its
The wind after three nights hurried away to its mother.

Спрашивала ветра мать:　„Где изволил пропадать?
[sprɑ́šyvɑlɑ v̡ɛ́trɑ mɑ́t̡　gd̡é‿izvól̡il　prɑpɑdɑ́t̡]
asked　wind　mother where did-[you]-deign　to-vanish
The mother asked the wind:　"Where have you disappeared to?

Али звёзды воевал?　Али волны всё гонял?"
[ɑ́l̡i z̡v̡ózdy vɑjɛvɑ́l ɑ́l̡i vólny　f̡s̡ó gɑn̡ɑ́l]
#　stars [you] fought　or　waves [you] kept driving
Have you been off fighting stars, or chasing waves?

„Не гонял я волн морских,　Звёзд не трогал золотых;
[n̡ɛgɑn̡ɑ́l jɑ vóln mɑrs̡k̡íx z̡v̡óst n̡ɛtrógɑl　zɑlɑtýx]
not-chased I　waves　of-sea　stars　did-not-touch　olden
I chased no sea waves, I touched no golden stars

Я дитя оберегал, колыбелечку качал!"
jɑ́ d̡it̡ɑ́ ɑb̡er̡ɛgɑ́l kɑlyb̡él̡eč̡ku kɑč̡ɑ́l]
I　child guarded　cradle　rocked
I was watching over a child, I was rocking its cradle.

*This text is in folk dialect.

11. Погоди!... 'Wait!...' Соч. 16, № 2

(N. Grekov) (1872)

Погоди! Для чего торопиться! Ведь и так жизнь несётся стрелой.
pagad̦í d̦l̦ač̦ɛvó tarap̦ítca v̦eț i tág‿žýz̦n̦ n̦eșótca șțr̦ɛlój]
wait why hurry indeed and thus life rushes like-arrow
Wait! Why hurry? Even as it is, life rushes past like an arrow.

Погоди! Погоди! Ты успеешь проститься, Как лучами восток загорится,
[pagad̦í pagad̦í ty ușp̦éjɛš prașțítca kak luč̦ám̦i vastóg‿zagar̦ítca]
wait wait you will-have-time to-say-goodbye as with-rays east will-light-up
Wait, wait! You will manage to say your farewells before the east lights up with the sun's rays.

Но дождёмся ль мы ночи такой? Посмотри, посмотри, как чудесно
[no dažd̦ómsal̦ my nóč̦i takój pasmațr̦í pasmațr̦í kak č̦ud̦ɛ́sna]
but will-see-again # we night such look look how wondrously
But will we ever again see such a night? Look, look how wondrously

Убран звёздами купол небесный! Как мечтательно смотрит луна!
[úbran z̦v̦ózdam̦i kúpal n̦eb̦ɛ́snyj kak m̦eč̦táțel̦na smóțr̦it luná]
adorned with-stars cupola of-sky how dreamy looks moon
Adorned with stars is the vault of the heavens, how dreamily the moon gazes at us!

Как темно в этой сени древесной, И какая везде тишина!
[kak țɛmnó vɛ́təj șɛ́n̦i d̦r̦ev̦ɛ́snəj i kakája v̦ez̦d̦ɛ́‿țišyná]
how dark in-this canopy arboreal and such everywhere quiet
How dark it is under this canopy of trees, and such stillness all around!

Только слышно, как шепчут берёзы, Да стучит сердце в пылкой груди...
[tól̦ka slýšna kakšɛ́pč̦ud‿b̦er̦ózy da stuč̦ít șɛ́rtcɛ fpýlkəj grud̦í]
only audible how whisper birches and pounds heart in-ardent breast
Only the whispering of the birches can be heard-- and a heart, pounding in an ardent breast!

Воздух весь полон запахом розы... Милый друг? Это жизнь, а не грёзы!
[vózdux v̦ɛ́ș pólan zápaxam rózy m̦ílyj drúk ɛ́ta žýz̦n̦ a n̦e g̦r̦ózy]
air all full of-smell of-rose dear friend this [is] life and not dreams
The air is filled with the scent of roses... My darling? This is really happening, not an illusion!

Жизнь летит... Погоди!
[žýz̦n̦ l̦ețít pagad̦í]
life is-flying wait
Life is rushing past, wait

12. Пойми хоть раз... 'Try to understand, just once...' Соч. 16, № 3 (A. Fet) (1872)

Пойми хоть раз тоскливое признанье,
[pajm̦í xoț rás tașk̦l̦ívaje‿p̦r̦iznán̦jɛ]
give-heed just once to-[my]-sad confession
Try to understand my sad confession at least this once,

Хоть раз услышь души молящей стон!
[xoț rás uslýš dušý mal̦áş̦ş̦ej stón]
just once hear of-soul imploring moan
Heed the moaning of my imploring soul.

Я пред тобой, прекрасное созданье,
já p̦r̦ɛttaboj p̦r̦ɛkrásnajɛ sazdán̦jɛ]
I before-you lovely creature
Before you, lovely creature, I

Безвестных сил дыханьем окрылён.
[b̦ɛzv̦ɛ́snyx șíl dyxán̦jɛm akryl̦ón]
of-unknown powers by-breath [am] winged
Am inspired by a breath of unknown strength.

Я образ твой ловлю перед разлукой,
[ja óbras tvój lav̦l̦ú p̦ɛr̦ɛdrazlúkəj]
I image your perceive before-parting
I drink in your image before we part;

Я полон им, немею и дрожу,--
[ja pólan ím n̦ɛm̦ɛ́ju i dražú]
I full of-it I-grow-dumb and tremble
I am filled with it, I grow mute and tremble.

И без тебя, томясь пред смертной мукой,
[i b̦ɛșțɛb̦á tam̦áș p̦r̦ɛtșm̦ɛ́rtnəj múkəj]
and without-you languishing before-mortal torment
And when you are gone, languishing in mortal torment,

Своей тоской, как счастьем, дорожу.
[șv̦ajéj taskoj kak ş̦ş̦áșțjɛm daražú]
my grief like happiness I-hold-dear
I revel in my grief as if it were happiness.

Пою её, во прах упасть готовый,
[pajú jejó vapráx upázd̦‿gatóvǝj]
I-sing it to-dust to-fall [I am]-ready
I proclaim it! I am ready to fall to my knees before you!

Ты предо мной стоишь, как божество.
[ty p̦r̦ɛdamnój staíš kag‿bažɛstvó]
you before-me stand like deity
You stand before me like a deity.

И я блажен: я в каждой муке новой
[i já blažɛ́n ja fkáždǝj múk̦ɛ nóvǝj]
and I [am] blessed I in-each torment new
And I am blessed. In every new torment

Твоей красы предвижу торжество.
[tvajéj krasý p̦r̦ɛdv̦ížu taržɛstvó]
of-your beauty I-foresee triumph
I foresee the triumph of your beauty.

13. О, спой же ту песню...* 'Oh, sing that song...' Соч. 16, № 4
(A. Pleshcheev, after Gimens) (1872)

О, спой же ту песню, родная, Что пела ты в прежние дни,
[o spój žɛ tú p̦éş̦n̦u radnája što p̦éla ty fp̦r̦ɛ́žn̦ije‿d̦n̦í]
oh sing # that song dearie that sang you in-former days.
Oh, sing that song, dearie, that you used to sing in days gone by.

В те дни, как ребёнком была я, Ты песенку вдруг запевала,
[fțé d̦n̦í kak r̦ɛbónkam bylá ja ty p̦éş̦ɛnku vdrúg‿zap̦ɛvála]
in-those days when child was I you song suddenly would-start-to-sing
In those days when I was only a child, suddenly you would break out in song,

И я на коленях твоих Под звуки той песни дремала.
[i já nakal̦ḙ́n̦ax tvaíx padzvúk̦i tój p̦éş̦n̦i d̦r̦ɛmála]
and I on-knees your at-sounds of-that song would-doze-off
And I, seated on your lap, would doze off to the sounds of your singing.

---

*These words are addressed by a woman to an older woman, the speaker's mother or nanny.

Ты пела, томима тоскою; Из тёмных, задумчивых глаз
[ty p̦éla tam̦íma taskóju isţómnyɣ‿zadúmç̦ivyɣ‿glás]
you sang tormented by-grief out-of-dark pensive eyes
You sang, although tormented by grief. From you dark pensive eyes

Катилась слеза за слезою…Протяжно и грустно ты пела…
[kaţílaş şļɛzá zaşļɛzóju praţážna i grúsna ty p̦ɛ́la]
would-roll tear after-tear at-length and sadly you would-sing
Would fall one tear after another. You would sing and sing, sad and long.

Любила напев я простой, Хоть слов я понять не умела…
[ļub̦íla nap̦ɛ́f ja prastój xoţ¯ slóf ja paņáţ ņɛum̦ɛ́la]
loved refrain I simple although words I to-understand was-not-able
I loved the simple refrain, although I couldn't understand the words.

О, спой же ту песню, родная, Как пела её в старину;
[o spój žɛ tu p̦ɛ́şņu radnája kak p̦ɛla jejó fstaŗinú]
oh sing # that song dearie as you-sang it in-old-days
Oh sing that song, dearie, as you sang it in days of yore,

Давно её смысл поняла я! И пусть под знакомые звуки
[davnó jejó smýsl paņalá ja i púşţ padznakómyjɛ zvúķi]
long-ago its sense came-to-understand I and may under-familiar sounds
I long since understand its message. And now let me, to the familiar sounds,

Убитая горем засну Я сном, что врачует все муки.
[ub̦ítaja góŗɛm zasnú ja snóm što vraç̦újɛt fşɛ́ múķi]
killed by-woe will-drift-off I in-sleep that heals all torments
Destroyed by adversity, drift off in a sleep that will heal all pain.

О, спой же ту песню, родная, Как пела её в старину!
[o spój žɛ tú p̦ɛ́şņu radnája kak p̦ɛla jejó fstaŗinú]
oh sing # that song dearie as you-sang it in-old-days
Oh, sing that song, dearie, as you sang it in days of yore,

О, спой же ту песнь! Спой же ту песнь, Как пела её в старину!
[o spój žɛ tú p̦ɛ́şņ spój žɛ tú p̦ɛ́şņ kak p̦ɛla jejó fstaŗinú]
oh sing # that song sing # that song as [you]-sang it in-old-days
Oh, sing that song, sing that song, as you sang it in days of yore.

14. Так что же 'And so what?' Соч. 16, № 5
(P. Tchaikovsky) (1872)

Твой образ светлый, ангельский и денно и нощно со мной;
[tvój óbras şv̧ɛ́tlyj ángɛl̨skəj i d̨ɛ́nna i nóş̧şna samnój]
your image fair angelic bothday and night [is] with-me
Your fair, angelic image is with me day and night--

И слёзы, и грёзы, и жуткие, страшные сны ты всё наполняешь собой!
[i şl̨ózy i gŗózy i žútķijɛ strášnyjɛ sný ty f̧şó napalņájɛš sabój]
and tears and dreams and awful terrible dreams you keep filling-up with-yourself
As well as tears, and reveries, and ghastly, terrible dreams that are filled with you.

Так что же? Что же? Хоть мучь, да люби!
[ták štó žɛ štó žɛ xaţ múç̧ da l̨uḑí]
so what # what # if-you-will torture but love
And so what? So what? Torment me, if you will, but love me!

Я тайну страсти пагубной глубоко хороню;
[ja tájnu strá̧şţi págubnəj glubóka xaraņú]
I secret of-passion baneful deeply conceal
I keep the secret of my baneful passion carefully hidden;

А ты коришь, стыдом язвишь!
[a ty kaŗíš stydóm jaz̧v̧íš]
but you reproach with-shame poison
And you only reproach me, you wound me by shaming me.

Ты только терзаешь меня безжалостной, грубой насмешкой!
[ty tól̨ka ţɛrzájɛš m̧eņá ḑɛžžálasnəj grúbəj naşm̧ɛ́škəj]
you only tear me with-merciless coarse ridicule
All you do is tear at me with your merciless, cruel ridicule.

Так что же? Что же? Терзай, да люби!
[ták štó žɛ štó žɛ ţɛrzáj da l̨uḑí]
so what # what # tear but love
And so what? So what? Tear at me, but love me!

Тебе до гроба верен я, но ты каждый день, каждый час
[ţeḑɛ́ dagróba v̧ɛ́ŗɛn ja no tý káždyj ḑɛ́ņ káždyj ç̧ás]
to-you until-grave true [am] I but you every day every hour
I am true to you till the grave, but you, every day, every hour,

Изменою яд в сердце льёшь, ты жизнь отравляешь мою!
[izm̡ɛ́naju ját fs̡ɛ́rtcɛ l̡jóš ty žýz̡n̡ atrav̡l̡ájɛš majú]
by-betrayal poison into-heart pour you life are-poisoning my
Poison my heart with your perfidy, you poison my entire life!

Нет, я не снесу этой муки! Нет жалости в сердце твоём!
[n̡ɛ́t ja n̡es̡n̡ɛsú ɛ́təj múk̡i n̡ɛ́d‿žálas̡t̡i fs̡ɛ́rtcɛ tvajóm]
no I will-not-bear this torment is-not pity in-heart your
No, I cannot bear this torment! Your heart knows no mercy!

Так что же? Что же? Убей, но люби!
[ták štó žɛ štó žɛ ub̡éj no l̡ub̡í]
so what # what# kill but love
And so what? So what? Kill me, but love me!

Убей меня, но люби!
[ub̡éj m̡en̡á no l̡ub̡í]
kill me but love
Kill me, but love me!

15. Новогреческая песнь (на тему „Dies irae") Соч. 16, № 6
'Neo-Greek Song (on the theme "Dies Irae")'
(A. Maikov) (1872)

В тёмном аде, под землёй, тени грешные томятся;
[ft̡ómnam ád̡ɛ padz̡em̡l̡ój t̡én̡i gr̡ɛ́šnyjɛ tam̡átca]
in-dark hell under-earth ghosts of-sinners languish
In dark Hell, under the Earth, souls of departed sinners are languishing.

Стонут девы, плачут жёны, и тоскуют, и крушатся…
[stónud‿d̡ɛ́vy pláčud‿žóny i taskújut i krušátca]
moan maidens weep wives and pine and grieve
Maidens are moaning, wives are weeping, all are pining away and grieving

Всё, всё о том, что не доходят вести в адские пределы, --
[fs̡ó fs̡ó atóm što n̡ɛdaxód̡at v̡és̡t̡i váts̡k̡ije‿p̡r̡ed̡ély]
all all about-that thatdoes-not-reach [them] news into-hell's peripheries
About the fact that no news reaches them in Hell of the world outside.

Жёны плачут, стонут: „Есть ли небо голубое?
[žóny pláçut stónut jéşţ ļi ņɛ́ba galubójɛ]
wives weep moan is-there # sky of-blue
The wives, weeping and moaning, ask: "Is there still a blue sky?

Есть ли свет ещё там белый!
[jéşţ ļi şvɛ́t jeşşó tám ḅɛ́lyj]
is-there # world still there of-white
Does God's Earth still exist?

Есть ли в свете церкви божьи и иконы золотые,
[jéşţ ļi fşvéţɛ cérkvi bóžji i ikóny zalatýjɛ]
is-there # in-world churches of-God and icons of-gold
Are there still churches to God and golden icons?

И, как прежде, за станками ткут ли девы молодые?“
[i kak pŗɛ́žḑɛ zastankáṃi tkút ļi ḑɛ́vy maladýjɛ]
and as before at-looms weave # maids young
And do young maidens still weave at looms, as formerly?

16. Уноси моё сердце... 'Bear my heart off...'

(A. Fet) (1872)

Уноси моё сердце в звенящую даль, Где, как месяц за рощей, печаль;
[unaşí majó şɛ́rtcɛ vzvenáşşuju dáļ gḑɛ kak ṃéşadz‿zaróşşej peçáļ]
bear-away my heart into-ringing distance where like moon beyond-grove sadness
Bear my heart off into the ringing distance where sadness reigns, like the moon beyond the grove.

В этих звуках на жаркие слёзы твои Кротко светит улыбка любви.
[véţiɣ‿zvúkax nažárķije‿şļózy tvaí krótka şvéţit ulýpka ļubví]
in-these sounds onto-hot tears your gently lights smile of-love
In these sounds, at your burning tears love gently smiles.

О дитя! Как легко средь незримых зыбей Доверяться мне песне твоей!
[o ḑiţá kak ļɛxkó şŗedņezŗímyɣ‿zyḅéj daveŗátca mņé‿ṗéşņɛ tvajéj]
oh child how easily among-invisible ripples to-trust for-me song your
Oh, child! How easy it is amidst the unseen ripples for me to believe in your song.

Выше, выше плыву серебристым путём,   Будто шаткая тень за крылом.
[výšɛ   výšɛ   plyvú şeŗeb̧ŗístym puţóm bútta šátkaja ţéņ   zakrylóm]
higher higher I-swim along-silvery path   as-if   unsteady shadow beyond-wing
Higher and higher I soar along the sivery path like the fluttering shadow of a wing in flight.

Вдалеке замирает твой голос, горя Словно за морем ночью заря.
[vdaļeķɛ́ zam̧irájɛt tvoj gólaz‿gaŗá   slóvna zámaŗɛm nóç̌ju   zaŗá]
in-distance dies-down   your   voice   burning like   beyond-sea at-night twilight
In the distance your voice subsides, aflame, just like dusk at sea.

И откуда-то вдруг, я понять не могу,
[i   atkúdata   vdrúk ja paņáţ   ņɛmagú
and from-somewhere suddenly I   understand cannot
And suddenly, from somewhere--I don't understand it!--

Грянет звонкий прилив жемчугу.
[ģŗáņɛd‿zvónkəj p̧ŗiļív‿žɛmç̌ugú]
bursts-forth sonorous surge   of-pearl
There bursts forth a resounding pearly surge.

Уноси ж моё сердце в звенящую даль, Где кротка, как улыбка, печаль,
[unaşí   ž majó şɛ́rtcɛ vz̧v̧eņáş̌ş̌uju dáļ   gḑɛ kratká kak ulýpka p̧eç̌áļ]
bear-away # my   heart   into-ringing   distance where gentle   like   smile [is] sadness
Bear my heart off into the ringing distance where sadness is as gentle as a smile;

И всё выше помчусь серебристым путём   Я, как шаткая тень за крылом.
[i   f̧şó výšɛ   pamç̌úş   şeŗeb̧ŗístym puţóm já kak šátkaja ţéņ   zakrylóm]
and ever higher I-will-rush along-silvery path   I   like   unsteady shadow beyond-wing
And ever higher I will soar along the silvery path like the fluttering shadow of a wing in flight.

17. Глазки весны голубые 'Little blue eyes of spring'

(M. Mikhailov, after Goethe)   (1873)

Глазки весны голубые   Кротко глядят из травы.
[gláşķi   v̧ɛsný   galubýjɛ krótka gļáḑat istravý]
little-eyes of-spring blue   meekly   gaze   out-of-grass
Spring's pale blue eyes are gazing meekly from the grass.

Любы вы милой, фиалки,-- С полем расстанетесь вы.
[ļúby   vy m̧íləj   f̧iálķi spóļɛm   rasstáņeţeş vý]
beloved [are] you to-[my]-dear-one violets with-field will-part   you
You violets are the favorites of my darling--you and this field must part.

Рву я цветы и мечтаю... В роще поют соловьи...
[rvú ja cv̡ɛtý i m̡ɛč̡táju vróš̡š̡ɛ pajút salav̡j̡í]
pick I flowers and daydream in-grove sing nightingales
I gather flowers and daydream. In the grove nightingales are singing.

Боже мой, кто рассказал им И думы и грёзы мои?
[bóžɛ moj któ rasskazál‿ym i dúmy i gr̡ózy maí]
God my who told them both thoughts and dreams my
Good heavens! Who told them all my thoughts and dreams?

Громко они распевают Всё, что на сердце таю...
[grómka an̡í rass̡p̡ɛvájut f̡s̡ó što nas̡ɛ́rtcɛ tajú]
loudly they sing all that in-heart I-conceal
Loudly they proclaim in song all that I conceal in my heart.

Целая роща узнала Нежную тайну мою.
[cɛ́laja róš̡š̡a uznála n̡ɛ́žnuju tájnu majú]
entire grove has-discovered tender secret my
The entire grove has discovered my tender secret.

18. Примиренье 'Reconciliation' Соч. 25, № 1
(N. Shcherbina) (1874)

О, засни, моё сердце, глубоко! Не буди, не пробудешь, что было,
[o zas̡n̡í majó s̡ɛ́rtcɛ glubóka n̡ɛbud̡í n̡ɛprabúd̡ɛš štó býla]
oh fall-sleep my heart deeply do-not-wake you-will-not-wake what was
Fall deeply asleep, my heart! Do not try, you cannot rewaken the past.

Не зови, что умчалось далёко, Не люби, что ты прежде любило...
[n̡ɛzav̡í štó umč̡álaz‿dal̡óka n̡ɛl̡ub̡í štó ty p̡r̡ɛ́žd̡ɛ‿l̡ub̡íla]
do-not-call what rushed-away far do-not-love what you formerly loved
Do not summon what has gone forever, do not try to love what you loved earlier.

Пусть надеждой и лживой мечтой Не смутится твой сон и покой.
[pús̡t̡ nad̡ɛ́ždəj i lžývəj m̡ɛč̡tój n̡ɛsmut̡ítca tvój són i pakój]
let by-hope and false dream not-become-muddied your sleep and quiet
Let your peace and quiet not be troubled by false hopes and dreams.

Для тебя невозвратно былое, На грядущее нет упованья...
[d̦l̦ațeb̦á n̦ɛvazvrátna bylójɛ nagr̦adúş̦şeje‿n̦ɛ́t upaván̦ja]
for-you irretrievable [is] past for-future is-not hope
The past is irretrievable, and there is no hope for the future...

Ты не знало в блаженстве покоя, Успокойся ж на ложе страданья
[ty n̦ɛznála vblažɛ́n̦șțv̦ɛ pakója uspakójsa ž nalóžɛ stradán̦ja]
you not-knew in-bliss peace be-at-peace therefore on-couch of-suffering
You found no peace in bliss; therefore be at peace on the couch of suffering.

И старайся не помнить зимой, Как срывало ты розы весной!
[i starájsa nɛpómn̦id̦‿z̦imój kak sryvála ty rózy v̦ɛsnój]
and try not-to-remember in-winter how picked you roses in-spring
And try not to recall in the winter how you gathered roses in the spring.

19. Как над горячею золой... 'As over burning coals...' Соч. 25, № 2
(F. Tiutchev) (1874)

Как над горячею золой Дымится свиток и сгорает,
[kak nadgar̦áç̦eju zalój dym̦ítca șv̦ítak i zgarájɛt]
as over-hot ashes smokes scroll and burns-up
As, over hot coals, a scroll first smokes and then is consumed,

И огнь, сокрытый и глухой, Слова и строки пожирает,--
[i ógn̦ sakrýtyj i gluxój slavá i strók̦i pažyrájɛt]
and flame secret and mute words and lines devours
And the flame, unseen and unheard, devours what is written there,

Так грустно тлится жизнь моя И с каждым днём уходит дымом;
[tag‿grúsna țl̦ítca žýz̦n̦ majá i skáždym d̦n̦óm uxód̦id‿dýmam]
so sadly smolders life my and with-each day leaves like-smoke
So does my life smolder away and with each day wafts away like smoke;

Так постепенно гасну я В однообразьи нестерпимом...
[tak pașțep̦ɛ́nna gásnu ja vadnaabráz̦ji n̦ɛșțɛr̦p̦ímam]
so gradually grow-dimmer I in-monotony unbearable
So do I gradually grow dimmer in unbearable monotony.

О небо, если бы хоть раз Сей пламень развился по воле,
[o n̡éba jéş|̡i by xaţ rás şéj plám̡en̡ razv̡ilsá pavó|̡ɛ]
oh heaven if would just once this flame develop according-to-[my]-will
Oh heaven! If only just once this flame could act as I would will it,

И, не томясь, не мучась доле, Я просиял бы и погас!
[i n̡ɛtam̡áş n̡ɛmúçaz‿dó|̡ɛ ja praşijál by i pagás]
and not-languishing not-suffering further I flare-up would and go-out
No longer languishing and suffering, I would flare up brightly once and then go out.

20. Песнь Миньоны 'Mignon's Song' Соч. 25, № 3
(F. Tiutchev, after Goethe) (1874)

Ты знаешь край, где мирт и лавр растёт, Глубок и чист лазурный неба свод,
[ty znájɛš kráj gd̡ɛ m̡írt‿y lávr raşţót glubók‿y çist lazúrnyj n̡éba svót]
you know land where myrtle and laurel grow deep and clean azure of-heaven vault
Do you know the land where myrtle and laurel grow? The azure vault of heaven is deep and pure.

Цветёт лимон, и апельсин златой, Как жар, горит под зеленью густой?...
[cv̡ɛţót |̡imón‿y ap̡e|̡şin zlatój kag‿žár gar̡ít padz̡é|̡en̡ju gustój]
blooms lemon and orange golden like glowing-embers burn under-greenery thick
There blooms the lemon tree, and oranges glitter like gold beneath lush greenery.

Ты знаешь край?... Туда, туда, туда с тобой Хотела б я укрыться, милый мой!...
[ty znájɛš kráj tudá tudá tudá stabój xaţéla b ja ukrýtca m̡ílyj mój]
you know land to-there with-you like would I hide-out dear my
Do you know the land? There, there, there with you I would like to take shelter, my dear one.

Ты знаешь высь, стезёй по крутизнам]
[ty znájɛš výş şţez̡ój pakruţiznám]
you know height [where] on-trail through-peaks
Do you know the heights where, along a trail among the peaks,

Лошак бредёт в тумане по скалам,
[lašág‿b̡red̡ót ftumán̡ɛ paskalám]
hinny makes-its-way in-mist along-cliffs
A hinny makes its way through the misty cliffs?

В ущельях гор отродье змей живёт,
[vuşşéļjaɣ‿gór atróḑje‿ẓṃéj žyỵót]
in-ravines of-mountains spawn of-serpents lives
In the ravines lives the spawn of serpents.

Гремит обвал, и водопад ревёт?
[gŗeṃít abvál i vadapát ŗeỵót]
thunders landslide and waterfall roars
Landslides thunder, and waterfalls roar.

Ты знаешь путь?... Туда, туда и нам с тобой проложен след:
[ty znájɛš púţ tudá tudá i nám stabój pralóžɛn şļɛ́t]
you know way to-there also for-us with-you [is] intended track
Do you know the way? The path is laid for you and me to go there.

Уйдём, властитель мой! Ты знаешь дом на мраморных столбах,
[ujḑóm vlaşţíţeļ mój ty znájɛž‿dóm namrámarnyx stalbáx]
let-us-leave lord my you know house on-marble columns
Let us depart, my lord! Do you know the house with marble columns?

Сияет зал, и купол весь в лучах; Глядят кумиры молча и грустя.
[sijájɛd‿zál i kúpal ỵéş vluçáx gļaḑát kuṃíry mólça i gruşţá]
shines hall and cupola all in-rays gaze idols silently and sadly
The hall is aglow and the cupola all radiant. Silent idols gaze out gloomily.

„Что, что с тобой, бедное дитя?“ Ты знаешь дом?...
[štó štó stabój ḅɛ́dnaje‿ḑiţá ty znájɛž‿dóm]
what what with-you poor child you know house
"What is wrong with you, my dear child?" Do you know the house?

Туда с тобой уйдём, родитель мой!
[tudá stabój ujḑóm raḑíţeļ mój]
to-there with-you let-us-leave parent my
Let us go there together, my father!

21. Канарейка 'The Canary'

(L. Mey)

Соч. 25, № 4
(1874)

Говорит султанша канарейке: „Птичка! Лучше в тереме высоком
[gavaŗít sultánša kanaŗéjķɛ ṗţíçka lútššɛ fţéŗeṃɛ vysókam]
says sultana to-canary birdie better in-tower-chamber tall
Said the sultana to the canary: "Little bird, is it not better here in this high tower-chamber

Щебетать и песни петь Зюлейке, Чем порхать на Западе далёком?
[ş̦ş̦eḅɛtáț i p̦éş̦ŋ̦i p̦éd̦¯ z̦uḷéjķɛ ç̦ɛm parxáț nazápad̦ɛ daḷókam]
to-chirp and songs sing to-Zuleika than to-flutter-about in-West distant
To twitter and sing songs to Zuleika, than to flutter around in the West far away?

Спой же, спой же мне про заморе, певичка,
[spój žɛ spój žɛ mŋ̦é prazámar̦e‿p̦ev̦íç̦ka]
sing # sing # to-me about-overseas little-singer.
Sing to me, sing to me of your distant land, little singer.

Спой же, спой же мне про Запад, непоседка!
[spój žɛ spój žɛ mŋ̦ɛ prazápat ŋ̦ɛpaş̦ɛ́tka]
sing # sing # to-me about-West restless-one
Sing to me, sing to me about the West, my fidgeter!

Есть ли там такое небо, птичка? Есть ли там такой гарем и клетка?
[jéş̦ț ḷi tám takóje‿ŋ̦éba p̦țíç̦ka jéş̦ț ḷi tám takój gar̦ém‿y ķḷɛ́tka]
is-there # there such sky bird is-there # there such harem and cage
Is there such a sky there, little bird? Is there such a harem there, such a fine cage?

У кого там столько роз бывало? У кого из шахов есть Зюлейка
[ukavó tám stóḷka róz‿byvála ukavó iššáxaf jéz̦d̦‿z̦uḷéjka]
by-whom there so-many roses were by-whom from-among-shahs is-there Zuleika
Who there ever had so many roses? Can any shah there boast of a Zuleika?

И поднять ли так ей покрывало?“ Ей в ответ щебечет канарейка:
[i padŋ̦áț ḷi ták jéj pakryvála jéj vatv̦ɛ́t ş̦ş̦eḅɛ́ç̦ɛt kanar̦éjka]
and to-raise # thus for-her veil to-her in-response chirps canary
And can she raise her veil so enticingly?” The canary chirped its response to her:

„Не проси с меня заморских песен, Не буди тоски моей без нужды:
[ŋ̦ɛpraş̦í smȩŋ̦á zamórş̦ķix p̦éşɛn ŋ̦ɛbud̦í taş̦ķí majéj ḅɛznúždy]
do-not-ask from-me overseas songs do-not-awake longing my needlessly
“Do not ask me for songs from overseas, do not awaken needlessly my longing for home.

Твой гарем по нашим песням тесен, И слова их одалискам чужды…
[tvój gar̦ém panášym p̦éş̦ŋ̦am țéşɛn i slavá ix adaḷiskam ç̦úždy]
your harem according-to-our songs [is] cramped and words their to-odalisques alien
Your harem is too cramped for our songs, and their words too alien to odalisques.

Ты в ленивой дрёме расцветала, Как и вся кругом тебя природа,
[ty vļeņívəj ḑŗóm̧ɛ rascvɛtála kák‿y fşá krugóm ţeb̧á p̧ŗiróda]
you in-lazy somnolence have-bloomed as also all around you nature
You have come into bloom here in drowsy indolence, just like your natural surroundings,

И не знаешь, даже не слыхала, Что у песни есть сестра -- свобода."
[i ņɛznájɛš dáže‿ņɛslyxála što up̧éşņi jéşţ şɛstrá svabóda]
and do-not-know even have-not-heard that by-song there-is sister freedom
And you do not know, you have never even heard, that Song has a sister called Freedom.

22. **Я с нею никогда не говорил... 'I never spoke with her...'** Соч. 25, № 5
(L. Mey) (1874)

Я с нею никогда не говорил, Но я искал повсюду с нею встречи,
[já sņéju ņikagdá ņɛgavaŗíl no já iskál paf̧şúdu sņéju f̧şţŗéçi]
I with-her never not-spoke but I sought everywhere with-her encounters
I never spoke with her, but I sought her out everywhere.

Бледнея и дрожа, за ней следил. Её движенья, взгляд, улыбку, речи
[b̧ļɛdņéja i dražá zaņéj şļeḑíl jejó ḑv̧ižéņja vzgļát ulýpku ŗéçi]
blanching and trembling after-her [I]-followed her movements glance smile utterances
Pale and trembling, I would follow her around. Her movements, glance, smile, words,

Я жадно, я внимательно ловил, А после я убегал от всех далече.
[ja žádna ja v̧ņimáţeļna lav̧íl a póşļe‿ja ub̧ɛgál atf̧şéɣ‿daļéçɛ]
I greedily I attentively took-in and afterward I ran-away from-everyone far
I greedily would drink in. And then I would run away to be by myself, far from everyone.

Её в мечтах себе я представлял, Грустил, вздыхал, томился и ревновал.
[jejó vm̧ɛçtáx şeb̧é‿ja p̧ŗɛtstav̧ļál gruşţíl vzdyxál tam̧ílsa i ŗɛvnavál]
her in-daydreams to-myself I imagined [I] grieved, sighed, languished and was-jealous.
I would imagine her before me, and I would grieve, sigh, languish and become jealous.

Не рассказать, что делалось со мною. Не описать волшебной красоты...
[ņɛrasskazáţ štó ḑélalaş samnóju ņɛap̧isáţ valšébnəj krasatý]
not-to-tell what happened with-me not-to-describe magic beauty
There are no words to relate what I went through, or to describe her magical beauty.

С весенним солнцем, с розовой зарёю, С слезой небес, упавшей на цветы,
[sv̡es̡én̡n̡im sóncɛm srózavəj zar̡óju ss̡l̡ɛzój n̡eb̡ɛ́s upáfšej nacv̡ɛtý]
with-spring sun with-rosy dawn with-tear of-heavens fallen onto-flowers
With the springtime sun, with the rosy dawn, with the tear from heaven that fell on the flowers,

С лучом луны, с вечернею звездою В моих мечтах слились её черты...
[sluč̡óm luný sv̡eč̡ɛ́rn̡eju z̡v̡ɛzdóju vmaíx m̡eč̡táx s̡l̡il̡is̡ jejó č̡ɛrtý]
with-ray of-moon with-evening star in-my daydreams fused her features
With the moonbeam, with the evening star, her features merged in all my reveries...

Я помню только светлое виденье, Мой идеал, отраду и мученье!
[ja pómn̡u tól̡ka s̡v̡étlaje‿v̡id̡én̡jɛ mój id̡ɛál atrádu i muč̡én̡jɛ]
I remember only fair vision my ideal delight and torment
I recall only a fair vision-- my ideal, my delight, my torment.

23. Как наладили: «Дурак...»* 'As they kept telling me: "Fool..."' Сой. 25, № 6
(L. Mey) (1874)

Как наладили: „Дурак, Брось ходить в царёв кабак!"
[kák nalád̡il̡i durák brós̡ xad̡ít̡ fcar̡óf kabák]
as [they]-told [me] fool stop to-go to-tsar's drinking-house
They kept telling me: "Fool, stop going to the state-owned tavern!"

Так и ладят всё одно: „Пей ты воду, не вино;
[ták‿y lád̡at fs̡ó adnó p̡éj ty vódu n̡ev̡inó]
thus # they-say repeatedly same drink you water not-wine
They keep saying the same thing: "Drink water, not wine!

Вон хошь речке поклонись, Хошь у быстрой поучись."
[vón xóš r̡éč̡k̡ɛ paklan̡ís̡ xóš ubýstrəj pauč̡ís̡]
there at-least to-river bow at-least from-rapid-one learn
Just go bow down to the river. Just learn a lesson from the fast-flowing one!"

Уж я к реченьке пойду, С речкой речи поведу:
[úš ja kr̡éč̡en̡k̡ɛ pajdú sr̡éč̡kəj r̡éč̡i pav̡ɛdú]
I to-river will-go with-river talks will-conduct
I guess I'll just go to the river and have a talk with her.

---

*This text is in folk dialect.

„Говорят мне: ты умна, -- Поклонюсь тебе до дна,
[gavaŗát mnɛ́ ty umná paklaņúş teb̧ɛ́ dadná]
they-say to-me you [are] wise I-will-bow to-you to-bottom
I'll say, "They tell me you're wise. I bow deeply before you.

Научи ты, как мне быть -- Пьянством люда не срамить?
[nauç̌í ty kák mnɛ́ býţ p̧jánstvam ļúda ņɛsram̧íţ
teach you how to-me to-be by-drunkeness people not-shame
Teach me how I should be, how not to shame people with my drunkeness;

Как в тебя, мою реку, Утопить змею-тоску?
[kák fţeb̧á majú ŗɛkú utap̧íḑ‿z̧m̧ejú taskú]
how in-you my river to-drown serpent melancholy
How to drown in you, oh river, the serpent of my melancholy.

А научишь -- век тогда Исполать тебе, вода,
[a naúç̌iš v̧ɛ́k tagdá ispaláţ¯ ţeb̧ɛ́ vadá]
and should-you-teach [me] forever then praise to-you water
If you can teach me, then praise to you forever, oh water,

Что отбила дурака От царёва кабака!“
[što adb̧íla duraká atcaŗóva kabaká]
that did-beat-away fool from-tsar's drinking-house
For driving a fool away from the state-owned tavern.

24. Хотел бы в единое слово... 'I wish I could in a single word...'
(L. Mey, after Heine) (1875)

Хотел бы в единое слово Я слить мою грусть и печаль
[xaţél by vjeḑínajɛ slóva ja şļíţ majú grúşţ i p̧eç̌áļ]
like would into-single word I to-fuse my grief and sadness
How I wish I could compress all my grief and sorrow into one word,

И бросить то слово на ветер, Чтоб ветер унёс его вдаль.
[i bróşiţ¯ tó slóva nav̧éţɛr štób v̧éţɛr uņós jɛvó vdáļ]
and to-throw that word into-wind so-that wind would-carry-off it into-distance
And then cast the word into the wind, so the wind could carry it far away.

И пусть бы то слово печали По ветру к тебе донеслось,
[i púz̧d͜by tó slóva p̧eçáļi pav̧étru kţeb̧é daņeslós̨]
and let # that word of-sadness on-wind to-you be-borne
And may that word of sadness be borne by the wind all the way to you,

И пусть бы всегда и повсюду Оно тебе в сердце лилось!
[i púz̧d͜by fs̨egdá i pafs̨údu anó ţeb̧é fs̨értcɛ ļilós̨]
and let # always and everywhere it to-you into-heart pour
And may the word pour into your heart, to remain there forever, wherever you go.

И если б усталые очи Сомкнулись под грёзой ночной,
[i jés̨ļi b ustályjɛ óçi samknúļis̨ padgŗózəj naçnój]
and if should [your] tired eyes close under-dream nocturnal
And should your tired eyes close for nocturnal reveries,

О пусть бы то слово печали Звучала во сне над тобой!
[o púz̧d͜by tó slóva p̧eçáļi zvuçála vas̨ņé nattabój]
oh let # that word of-sadness sound in-dreams over-you
May that word of sadness ring in your dreams.

25. Недолго нам гулять... 'We haven't long to stroll...'

(N. Grekov) (1875)

Недолго нам гулять рука с рукой в саду густом,
[ņɛdólga nám guļáţ ruká srukój fsadú gustóm]
not-for-long for-us to-stroll hand in-hand in-garden lush
We do not have long to stroll hand in hand in the lush garden,

По липовым аллеям, при блеске звёзд,
[paļípavym aļéjam p̧ŗib̧ļés̨k̨e͜z̧v̧óst]
along-linden lanes by-light of-stars
Along lanes of lindens in the starlight

Вечернею порой, и жизнь разнеженной душой
[v̧eçérņeju parój i žýz̧ņ razņéžɛnnəj dušój]
in-evening time and life by-deeply-moved soul
At evening time, and to thank life with our souls, deeply moved,

Благодарить за всё, что мы имеем. Недолго нам под обаяньем снов,
[blagadaŗíţ zafs̨ó što mý im̧éjɛm ņɛdólga nám padabajáņjɛm snóf]
to-thank for-all that we possess not-long to-us under-charm of-dreams
For all that we possess. We do not have long, under the spell of dreams,

Как молодость, игривых и летучих, Следя луну в изгибах облаков,
[kák móladaşţ igŗívyx‿y ļɛtúçix şļeḑá lunú vyzg̡íbax ablakóf]
like youth playful and fleeting following moon in-crevices of-clouds
Which are as playful and fleeting as youth, following the moon in and out of the clouds,

Мечтать о том, чему нет слов, Но что живёт в душах у нас кипучих.
[m̡eçţáţ atóm çɛmú ŋ̡ɛ́t slóf nó štó žyɣód‿vdušáx unás ķipúçix]
to-dream of-that for-which is-not words but which lives in-souls by-us turbulent
To dream about that for which no words exist, but which lives in our restless souls.

О милый друг! Цвести недолго Нам блаженством чувств!
[o m̡ílyj drúk cɣeşţí ŋ̡ɛdólga nám blažɛ́nstvam çústf]
oh dear friend to-bloom not-long to-us by-bliss of-feelings
Oh, dear friend! We are not given long to flourish in the bliss of feelings!

Зато мы долго будем за них Судьбе страданьем дань нести
[zató mý dólga búḑɛm zaŋ̡íx suḑb̡ɛ́ stradáŋ̡jɛm dáŋ̡ ŋ̡eşţí]
however we long will for-them to-fate by-suffering tribute bear
Moreover we shall by our suffering long do homage to fate for having had these feelings,

И слова страшного „прости!“ Мы никогда с тобой не позабудем.
[i slóva strášnava praşţí mý ŋ̡ikagdá stabój ŋ̡ɛpazabúḑɛm]
and word terrible farewell we never with-you we-will-not-forget
And the terrible word "Farewell" you and I will never forget.

26. На сон грядущий 'At bedtime' Соч. 27, №
(N. Ogarev) (1875)

Ночная тьма безмолвие приносит И к отдыху зовёт меня.
[naçnája ţmá b̡ɛzmólɣije‿p̡ŗinóşit i kóddyxu zaɣót m̡eŋ̡á]
nocturnal gloom silence brings and to-rest calls me
The silence of the night brings peace and summons me to rest.

Пора, пора! покоя тело просит, Душа устала в вихре дня.
[pará pará pakója ţéla próşit dušá ustála vɣíxŗe‿ḑŋ̡á]
time time rest body begs-for soul has-grown-tired in-whirlwind of-day
It is time, it is time. My body aches for quiet, my soul has grown weary in the bustle of the day.

Молю тебя пред сном грядущим, Боже: „Дай людям мир,
[maḽú ţeḅá pṛɛtsnóm gṛadúş̧ş̧im bóžɛ dáj ḽúḑam ṃír]
I-beseech Thee before-sleep approaching God give to-people peace
God, I beseech Thee before going to sleep: Grant Thy people peace,

Благослови младенца сон и нищенское ложе, И слёзы тихие любви!
[blagaslaṿí mlaḑénca són i ņíş̧ş̧ɛnskajɛ lóžɛ i ş̧ḽózy ţíxije‿ḽubṿí]
bless of-baby dreams and beggar's couch and tears quiet of-love
Bless the sleep of babes, the couch of the destitute, and the quiet tears shed in the name of love!

Прости греху, на жгучее страданье Успокоительно дохни,
[praşţí gṛɛxú nažgúç̧ejɛ stradáņjɛ uspakaíţeḽna daxņí]
forgive sin onto-burning suffering soothingly breathe
Forgive sin and send Thy cooling breath to assuage burning suffering

И все твои печальные созданья Хоть сновиденьем обмани!
[i fş̧é tvaí ṗeç̧áḽnyjɛ sazdáņja xoţ snaṿiḑéņjɛm abmaņí]
and all thy sad creatures at-least with-dream deceive
And by sending pleasant dreams give at least fleeting hope to all Thy sad creatures.

27. Смотри: вон облако... 'Look at yonder cloud...'

Соч. 27, № 2 (1875)

(N. Grekov)

Смотри: вон облако несётся серебристое;
[smaţṛí vón óblaka ņeşótca şeṛeḅŗístajɛ]
look there cloud speeds-along silvery
Look at that silvery cloud racing past;

Везде вокруг него сияет небо чистое,
[ṿeẓḑé vakrukņɛvó şijájɛt ņéba ç̧ístajɛ]
everywhere around-it shines sky clean
All around it the clear sky is aglow,

Как молодость прекрасная твоя.
[kák móladaşţ ṗṛɛkrásnaja tvajá]
like youth lovely your
Like your lovely youthfulness.

И утра блеск на нём так ярко отражается;
[i útra b̦l̦ésk nan̦óm tak járka atražájɛtca]
and morning's gleam on-it so brightly is-reflected
And the morning's gleam on it is so brightlty reflected;

И так оно светло, как будто улыбается.
[i ták anó șv̦ɛtló kag‿bútta ulybájɛtca]
and so it light as if it-smiles
And it shines so, as if it were smiling.

Оно похоже на тебя.
[anó paxóžɛ națeb̦á]
it looks-like you
It is like you.

Смотри: вон туча там выходит одинокая;
[smațr̦í vón túç̦a tám vyxód̦it ad̦inókaja]
look yon storm-cloud there is-emerging solitary
Look, over there a solitary storm cloud has apppeared;

Она темна, как ночь, как грусть души глубокая.
[aná țɛmná kak nóç̦ kag‿grúz̦d̦‿dušý glubókaja]
it [is] dark as night like grief of-soul deep
It is as dark as night, like the profound melancholy of the soul.

Не просветлит её сиянье дня
[n̦ɛprașv̦ɛtl̦ít jejó șijáņje‿d̦n̦á]
will-not-shed-light on-it shining of-day
The day's brightness will shed no light on it.

Быть может, оттого она мрачна так, грозная,
[býț móžɛt attavó aná mraç̦ná tag‿gróznaja]
it-to-be could from-that it [is] dark so threatening
Perhaps it is so dark and ominous because of the fact

Что с светлым облаком дана стезя ей розная, --
[što șșv̦étlym óblakam daná șțez̦á jéj róznaja]
that with-bright cloud is-given path to-it varying
That it has been destined to follow a path different from that of the light cloud.

Она похожа на меня.
[aná paxóža nam̡en̡á]
it looks-like me
It is like me.

28. Не отходи от меня... 'Do not leave me...' Соч. 27, № 3
(A. Fet) (1875)

Не отходи от меня, друг мой, останься со мной!
[n̡ɛatxad̡í atm̡en̡á drúk mój astán̡sa samnój]
do-not-withdraw from-me friend my stay with-me
Don't leave me, my friend, stay with me.

Не отходи от меня: мне так отрадно с тобой...
[n̡ɛatxad̡í atm̡en̡á mn̡ɛ ták atrádna stabój]
do-not-withdraw from-me to-me so joyous with-you
Don't leave me--I am so happy with you.

Ближе друг к другу, чем мы,-- Ближе нельзя нам и быть;
[b̡l̡ížɛ drúg‾‿gdrúgu č̡ém mý b̡l̡ížɛ‿n̡el̡z̡á nám‿y být̡]
closer one to-another than we closer it-is-impossible for-us # to-be
Closer to one another than we are--closer we could not be.

Чище, живее, сильней Мы не умеем любить.
[č̡íš̡š̡ɛ žyv̡éje‿s̡il̡n̡éj my n̡ɛum̡éjɛm l̡ub̡ít̡]
purer livelier stronger we do-not-know-how to-love
We are incapable of loving any more purely, truly, strongly.

Если же ты предо мной, Грустно головку склоня,--
[jés̡l̡i žɛ tý p̡r̡ɛdamnój grúsna galófku sklan̡á
if # you [are] before-me sadly little-head bending-down
If you stand before me, your head sadly bowed--

Мне так отрадно с тобой... Не отходи от меня!
[mn̡ɛ́ tak atrádna stabój n̡ɛatxad̡í atm̡en̡á]
to-me so joyous with-you do-not-withdraw from-me
I am so happy with you... Don't leave me!

29. Вечер* 'Evening' Соч. 27, № 4
(L. Mey, after Shevchenko) (1875)

Вишнёвый садик возле хаты; Жуки над вишнями гудят;
[v̧išņóvyj sáḑik voz̧ļɛxáty žuķí nadv̧íšņam̧i guḑát]
cherry orchard [is] beside-hut beetles over-cherry-trees hum
There is a little cherry orchard beside the hut. Beetles hum over the treetops.
Плуг с нивы пахари тащат; И, распеваючи, девчаты
[plúk sņívy páxaŗi taş̧şát i rasp̧ɛvájuç̌i ḑɛfç̧áty]
plow from-field plowmen drag and singing girls
Plowmen are hauling the plow in from the field, and, singing, girls

Домой на вечерю спешат. Семья их ждёт, и всё готово;
[damój nav̧éç̌eŗu ş̧p̧ɛšát şem̧já iɣ‿žḑót i f̧şó gatóva]
home o-supper hurry family them awaits and all [is] ready
Hurry home to their evening meal. The family awaits them, and all is ready.

Звезда вечерняя встаёт, И дочка ужин подаёт.
[z̧v̧ɛzdá v̧eç̌ɛrņaja fstajót i dóç̌ka úžyn padajót]
star of-evening rises and daughter supper serves
The evening star appears, and the daughter serves up supper.

А мать сказала бы ей слово Да соловейка не даёт.
[a máţ skazála by jéj slóva da salav̧éjka ņɛdajót]
and mother say would to-her word but nightingale does-not-permit
Mother wants to say something to her, but the nightingale won't let her.

Мать уложила возле хаты Малюток деточек своих;
[máţ ulažýla voz̧ļɛxáty maļútag‿ḑévačɛk svaíx]
mother has-laid alongside-hut youngsters children her
Mother has put the little children down to sleep beside the hut.

Сама заснула возле них… Затихло всё… одни девчаты
[samá zasnúla voz̧ļɛņíx zaţíxla f̧şó adņí ḑɛfç̧áty]
she-herself dozes-off beside-them has-grown-quiet all only girls
Mother herself goes to sleep beside them. All is still. Only the girls

Да соловейка не затих.
[da salav̧éjka ņɛzaţíx]
and nightingale have-not-grown-silent
And the nightingale have not been able to settle down.

---

*This text is in folk dialect.

30. Али мать меня рожала...* 'Why was I born?' Соч. 27, № 5
(L. Mey, after Mickiewicz) (1875)

Али мать меня рожала на горе большое?
[aļi máţ meņá ražála nagoŗé baļšóje]
\# mother me bore for-woe great
Did my mother give birth to me only so that I could suffer so?

Али ведьма зачурала мне гнездо родное?
[aļi védma začurála mņé gņezdó radnóje]
or witch cursed to-me nest home
Or did a witch put a curse on my home nest?

Напролёт и дни и ночи плачу, как ребёнок;
[napraļót‿y dņí i nóči pláču kak ŗebónak]
straight-through both days and nights I-weep like child
I weep like a child all day and all night.

Сваты придут -- нет мне мочи выстоять смотрёнок.
[sváty pŗídut ņét mņe móči vystajáţ smaţŗónak]
matchmakers will-come is-not to-me power to-endure inspection
Whenever matchmakers come I cannot bear to submit to being inspected.

Ох, уехал да и сгинул милый за дружиной;
[óx ujéxal da i zgínul mílyj zadružýnəj]
ah he-lef # and vanished dear-one after-army
Ah, my dear one has gone away with the army and vanished.

Не сберёг -- одну покинул панночку с кручиной.
[ņezbeŗók adnú pakínul pánnačku skručínəj]
he-did-not-safeguard alone he-deserted girl with-sorrow
He left a maid alone with her sorrow.

У подружек в церкви ясно свечка догорает;
[upadrúžek fcérkvi jásna şvéčka dagarájet]
by-girlfriends in-church clearly candle burns-down
In church my girlfriends' candles burn brightly all the way down.

---

*This text is in folk dialect.

У меня одной, несчастной, сразу погасает.
[um̡en̡á adnój n̡eš̡š̡ásnəj srázu pagasájɛt]
by-me alone wretched-one immediately goes-out
Only my candle, alas, goes out immediately.

В поле осень; лист валится, пёс наш землю роет;
[fpól̡ɛ ós̡en̡ l̡ist val̡ítca p̡ós naž‿z̡ém̡l̡u rójɛt]
in-field autumn leaf falls dog our [in]-earth roots
Fall has come, the leaves are falling. Our dog roots in the earth.

Сыч на крышу к нам садится: „Что ж ты, скоро?“ воет.
[sýč̡ nakrýšu knám sad̡ítca štóš tý skóra vójɛt]
owl on-roof to-us sits what you soon it-howls
An owl perches on our roof and hoots at me: "Well, will your time come soon?"

Скоро я с тобою, значит, свижуся, мой милый!
[skóra já stabóju znáč̡it s̡v̡ížusa mój m̡ílyj]
soon I with-you it-means will-meet my darling
It means that I will soon be with you again, my darling.

31. Моя баловница (2-я редакция) — Соч. 27, № 6
'My naughty girl (2d edition)'

(L. Mey, after Mickiewicz) (1875)

Моя баловница, отдавшись веселью,
[majá balovn̡íca addáfšys̡ v̡es̡él̡ju]
my naughty-girl being-given to-merriment
My naughty girl, being given to merriment,

Зальётся, как птичка, серебряной трелью,
[zal̡jótca kak p̡t̡íč̡ka s̡er̡éb̡ranəj t̡r̡él̡ju]
will-pour-forth like bird with-silvery trill
Will burst forth in a silvery trill like a songbird,

Как птичка, начнёт щебетать, лепетать,
[kak p̡t̡íč̡ka nač̡n̡ót š̡š̡eb̡ɛtát̡ l̡ep̡ɛtát̡]
like bird will-begin to-twitter to-chatter
Like a bird, will suddenly begin to twitter and chatter,

Так мило начнёт лепетать, щебетать,
[tak m̡ila naç̡n̡ót l̡ep̡εtát̡ ş̡ş̡eb̡εtát̡]
so sweetly will-begin to-chatter to-twitter
So sweetly will begin to chatter and twitter

Что даже дыханьем боюсь я нарушить
[što dážε dyxán̡jεm bajúş̡ ja narúšyd̡‿]
that even by-breathing fear I to-violate
That I am afraid to breathe, lest I disrupt

Гармонию сладкую девственных слов,
[garmón̡iju slátkuju d̡éfş̡t̡v̡εnnyx slóf]
harmony sweet of-girlish words
The sweet harmony of her girlish words;

И целые дни, и всю жизнь я готов
[i célyje d̡n̡í i f̡ş̡ú žýz̡n̡ ja gatóf]
and entire days and whole life I [am] ready
And for days on end, for a lifetime, I am willing

Красавицу слушать и слушать.
[krasáv̡icu slúšat̡ i slúšat̡]
beauty to-listen-to and to-listen-to
To listen and listen to my darling.

Когда ж живость речи ей глазки зажжёт,
[kagdá ž žývaşt̡ r̡éç̡i jej gláşk̡i zaž̡ž̡ót]
when # liveliness of-speech to-her eyes will-light-up
Whenever her eyes begin to sparkle from her lively speech,

И щёки сильнее румянить начнёт,
[i ş̡ş̡ók̡i şil̡n̡éjε rum̡án̡it̡ naç̡n̡ót]
and cheeks more-strongly to-redden will-begin
And her cheeks begin to flush,

Когда при улыбке, сквозь алые губы,
[kagdá p̡r̡iulýpk̡ε skvoz̡ álýjε gúby]
when upon-smiling through scarlet lips
Whenever, in smiling, through her scarlet lips

Как перлы в коралах, блеснут её зубы,
[kak pérly fkarálax bļɛsnút jejó zúby]
like pearls in-coral will-gleam her teeth
Like pearls against coral, her teeth glisten,

О, в эти минуты я смело опять
[o véţi mịnúty ja şmɛ́la apáţ]
oh in-these minutes I boldly again
Oh, at such times again I boldly

Гляжуся ей в очи и жду поцелуя,
[gļažúsa jej vóçi i ždú pacɛlúja]
I-look-at-myself to-her in-eyes and await kiss
I gaze into her eyes and wait for her kiss,

И более слушать её не хочу я,
[i bóļejɛ slúšaţ jejó ņɛxaçú ja]
and further to-listen to-her do-not-want I
And I no longer want to listen to her,

А всё целовать, целовать, целовать.
[a fşó cɛlaváţ cɛlaváţ cɛlaváţ]
but just to-kiss to-kiss to-kiss
But rather to kiss her and kiss her and kiss her.

Мою баловницу всю жизнь я готов
[majú balavņícu fşú žýẓņ ja gatóf]
my spoiled-girl all life I [am] ready
My spoiled girl, I am ready for a whole lifetime

Целовать, целовать, целовать.
[cɛlaváţ cɛlaváţ cɛlaváţ]
to-kiss to-kiss to-kiss
To kiss and kiss and kiss.

32. Нет, никогда не назову... 'No, I will never name her...' Соч. 28, № 1
(N. Grekov, after Musset) (1875)

Нет, никогда вам не узнать, кого люблю я.
[ņét ņikagdá vám ņɛuznáţ kavó ļuḅļú ja]
no never for-you not-to-learn whom love I
No, you are never to discover who it is that I love.

За всю вселенную её не назову я.
[zafşú fşeļénnuju jejó ņɛnazavú ja]
for-whole universe her will-not-name I
Not for the entire universe would I tell you her name.

Давайте петь! и будет вам мой вторить голос,
[davájţe‿ pét i búdɛt vám mój ftóŗiḑ‿gólas]
let-us sing and will to-you my to-sing-along voice
Let us sing! And my voice will second yours in song about her:

Что белокурая она, как зрелый колос;
[što ḅɛlakúraja aná kag‿zŗélyj kólas]
that fair-haired [is] she as ripe ear-of-grain
That her hair is as golden as ripe grain,

Что воли ни за что её я не нарушу,
[što vóļi ņizaštó jejó ja ņɛnarúšu]
that will not-for-anything her I would-not-violate
That I would never go against her will

И, коль захочет, ей отдам всю жизнь и душу.
[i kóļ zaxóçɛt jéj addám fşú žýzņ i dúšu]
and if she-should-want to-her I-would-give all life and soul
And would give her my life and soul, if she desired.

Я муки пламенной любви от ней скрываю:
[ja múķi plaṃɛnnəj ļubýi atņéj skryváju]
I torments of-flaming love from-her conceal
I keep the torments of my ardent love a secret from her.

Они не сносны, и от них я умираю.
[aņí ņɛsnósny i atņíx ja uṃiráju]
they [are] unbearable and from-them I am-dying
They are unbearable and are destroying me.

Но кто она…
[no któ aná]
but who [is] she
But who is she?…

Нет, я люблю её, люблю с такою силой,
[ņɛ́t ja ļub̦ļú jejó ļub̦ļú stakóju şíləj]
no I love her love with-such power
No, I love her, love her so very much,

Что пусть умру, но не скажу я имя милой.
[što púşţ umrú no ņɛskažú ja ím̦a m̦íləj]
that may I-die but will-not-say I name of-beloved
That I would die before I would tell you the name of my beloved.

33. Корольки 'Coral Beads' Соч. 28, № 2
(L. Mey, after Syrokomla) (1875)

Как пошёл я с казаками, Ганна говорила:
[kák pašól ja skazakám̦i gánna gavaŗíla]
as set-off I with-Cossacks Hannah said
As I was leaving with the Cossacks, Hannah said to me:

«За тебя я со слезами Бога умолила:
[zaţeb̦á ja saşļɛzám̦i bóga umaļíla]
for-you I with-tears God have-implored
"With tears flowing, I have begged God to care for you,

Ты вернёшься с первой битвы весел и здоров,--
[ty v̦eŗņóšsa sp̦érvəj b̦ítvy v̦éşɛl‿y zdaróf]
you will-return from-first battle happy and healthy
That you will return safe and happy from you first battle.

Привези ж мне за молитвы нитку корольков!»
[p̦ŗiv̦ez̦í ž mņɛ́ zamaļítvy ņítku karaļkóf]
bring # to-me for-prayers string of-coral-beads
In return for my prayers, bring me back a string of coral beads."

Бог послал нам атамана: сразу мы разбили
[bóx paslál nám atamána srázu my razb̦íļi]
God sent to-us ataman right-away we smashed
God sent us a good ataman: quickly we defeated

В пух и прах всё войско хана, город полонили,
[fpúx‿y práx fşó vójska xána górat palaņíļi]
to-smithereens # while army of-khan city took-prisoner
Totally the Khan's whole army and took the city captive.

Сбили крепкие ворота, пир для казаков!
[zbíļi ķŗέpķijε varóta pír dļakazakóf]
we-tore-down strong gates feast for-Cossacks
We ripped down the strong gates. Feast-time for the Cossacks!

У меня одна забота: нитка корольков!
[umeņá adná zabóta ņítka karaļkóf]
by-me one concern string of-coral-beads
I had but one concern: the string of coral beads.

Вдруг сама в глаза блеснула,-- знать, помог всевышний--
[vdrúk samá vglazá bļεsnúla znáţ pamók fşεvýšņij]
suddenly it-itself in-eyes shone clearly helped Almighty
Suddenly there they were, shining before my eyes--surely the Almighty had intervened!--

И сама мне в горсть юркнула алой крупной вишней.
[i samá mņέ vgóŗşţ jurknúla áləj krúpnəj víšņej]
andit-itself to-me into-hand plunged like-scarlet giant cherries
And they fell into my hand like big scarlet cherries.

Я добычу крепко стиснул да и был таков:
[ja dabýçu ķŗépka şţísnul da i býl takóf]
I loot firmly clutched # andwas such
I grasped the treasure firmly and made off with it.

Прямо к Ганне степью свистнул с ниткой корольков.
[pŗáma ggánņe şţépju şvísnul sņítkəj karaļkóf]
straight to-Hannah through-steppesnuck with-stringof-coral-beads
Away I sped across the steppe to my Hannah, coral beads in hand,

И не спрашивал я брода, гати или моста...
[i ņεsprášyval ja bróda gáţi iļi mósta]
anddid-not-ask-about I ford road or bridge
Not pausing to ask anyone for information along the way.

Звон у нашего прихода: люд валит с погоста…
[zvón unášɛva p̡r̡ixóda l̡út val̡ít spagósta]
tolling at-our arrival people thronging from-graveyard
Bells were tolling when we arrived, with people flocking from the graveyard.

И кричит мне вся громада сотней голосов:
[i k̡r̡ič̡ít mn̡ɛ f̡s̡á gramáda sótn̡ej galasóf]
and cries to-me whole multitude in-hundred voices
And the whole throng shouted to me, a hundred voices strong:

«Ганна там -- и ей не надо нитки корольков!»
[gánna tám i jéj n̡ɛnáda n̡ítk̡i karal̡kóf]
Hannah [is] there and to-her not-needed string of-coral-beads
"Hannah lies yonder and no longer has need of coral beads."

Сердце сжалось, замирая, в груди раздроблённой,
[s̡ɛ́rtcɛ žžálaz̡‿zam̡irája vgrud̡í razdrab̡l̡ónnəj]
heart compressed stopping-beating in-chest shattered
My heart sank, stopped beating in my shattered breast.

И упал с коня, рыдая, я пред иконой!
[i upál skan̡á rydája ja p̡r̡ɛdykónəj]
and fell from-horse sobbing I before-icon
And sobbing, I fell from my horse before the holy icon.

О пощаде я молил без слов
[apaš̡š̡ád̡e‿ja mal̡íl b̡ɛsslóf]
for-mercy I prayed without-words
I prayed wordlessly for her soul

И повесил на окладе нитку корольков.
[i pav̡és̡il naaklád̡ɛ n̡ítku karal̡kóf]
and hung on-frame string of-coral-beads
And hung on the icon's frame the string of coral beads.

34. Зачем? 'Why?' Соч. 28, № 3
(L. Mey) (1875)

Зачем же ты приснилася, красавица далёкая,
[zaçém žɛ tý pŗişņílasa krasáyica daļókaja]
why # you appeared-in-dream beauty distant
Why have you come to me in a dream, lovely one far away,

И вспыхнула, что в полыме, подушка одинокая?
[i fspýxnula što fpólyme padúška adinókaja]
and has-flared-up as in-flame pillow lonely
And set my lonely pillow ablaze, as if in flames?

Ох, сгинь ты, полуночница!
[ox zgiņ ty polunóçņica
oh vanish you night-person
Oh, be gone, nocturnal apparition!

Глаза твои ленивые и пепел кос рассыпчатый,
[glazá tvaí ļeņívyjɛ i pépɛl kós rassýpçatyj]
eyes your langurous and ashes of-plaits crumbly
Your langurous eyes and your fair hair, falling loose,

И губы горделивые,-- всё наяву мне снилося,
[i gúby gaŗdeļívyjɛ fşó najavú mņe‿şņílasa]
and lips proud everything as-alive to-me appeared-in-dream
And your proud lips--everything in the dream was as real as life,

И всё, что грёза вешняя, умчалося,-- и на сердце
[i fşó što gŗóza yéšņaja umçálasa i náşɛrtcɛ]
and everything as dream spring rushed-off and into-heart
And then, like a daydream in spring, everything vanished--and in my heart

Легла потьма кромешная!
[ļɛglá paţmá kraméšnaja]
lay darkness total
Lay only pitch blackness!

Зачем же ты приснилася, красавица далёкая,
[zaçém žɛ tý pŗişņílasa krasáyica daļókaja]
why # you appeared-in-dream beauty distant
Why have you come to me in a dream, lovely one far away,

Коль стынет вместе с грёзою подушка одинокая?
[kólʲ stýnʲɛt vmʲéstʲɛ zgrʲózaju padúška adʲinókaja]
if will-cool-down together with-dream pillow lonely
Since, along with the dream, my lonely pillow will again grow cold.

35. Он так меня любил... 'He loved me so...' Соч. 28, № 4
(D. de Girardin. Translated by A. Apukhtin [?]) (1875)

Нет, не любила я! Но странная забота
[nʲét nʲelʲubʲíla ja no stránnaja zabóta]
no did-not-love I but strange worry
No, I did not love him! But a strange uneasiness,

Теснила грудь мою, когда он приходил;
[tʲesnʲíla grútʲ majú kagdá on prʲixadʲíl]
pressed breast my when he arrived
A tightness would arise in my breast whenever he arrived.

То вся краснела я, боялася чего-то,--
[to fsʲá krasnʲéla ja bajálasa čʲɛvóta]
then all blush I feared something
Then I would blush all over, as if I were afraid of something--

Он так меня любил, он так меня любил!
[ón ták mʲenʲá lʲubʲíl ón ták mʲenʲá lʲubʲíl]
he so me loved he so me loved
He loved me so much, he loved me so much!

Чтоб нравиться ему тогда, цветы и те наряды
[štob nrávʲitca jɛmú tagdá cvʲetý i tʲɛ́ narʲády]
in-order to-please him then flowers and that finery
In order to be attractive to him at that time, flowers and finery

Я берегла, что он по сердцу находил;
[já bʲerʲɛglá što on pasʲértcu naxadʲíl]
I valued that he to-heart found
I put great store in--whatever pleased his heart.

С ним говорила я, его ловила взгляды --
[snʲím gavarʲíla ja jɛvó lavʲíla vzglʲády]
with-him talked I his would-seek glances
I would talk to him often and try to catch his eye--

Он так меня любил, он так меня любил!
[ón ták m̡en̡á l̡ub̡íl ón ták m̡en̡á l̡ub̡íl]
he so me loved he so me loved
He loved me so much, he loved me so much!

Но раз он мне сказал: «В ту рощу в час заката
[no rás ón mn̡ɛ́ skazál ftú róš̡š̡u fč̡áz‿zakáta]
but once he to-me said to-that thicket at-hour of-dusk
But once he said to me: "That thicket, at dusk--

Придёшь ли?» --«Да, приду!» Но не хватило сил.
[p̡r̡id̡óš l̡i dá p̡r̡idú no n̡ɛxvat̡íla s̡íl]
will-you-come # yes I-will-come but did-not-suffice strength
Will you come?" "Yes, I'll come!" But I lacked the will.

Я в рощу не пошла, он ждал меня напрасно!
[ja vróš̡š̡u n̡ɛpašlá ón ždál m̡en̡á naprásna]
I to-thicket did-not-gohe awaited me in-vain
I didn't go to that thicket, he waited for me in vain

Тогда уехал он, сердясь на неудачу;
[tagdá ujɛ́xal ón s̡er̡d̡ás̡ nan̡ɛudáč̡u]
then left he being-angry at-failure
And so he went away, angry about his failure.

Несчастный, как меня проклясть он должен был!
[n̡eš̡š̡ásnyj kák m̡en̡á prak̡l̡ás̡t̡ ón dólžɛn býl]
unfortunate how me to-curse he should have
Poor man! How he must have cursed me!

Я не увижусь с ним, мне тяжело, я плачу…
[já n̡ɛuv̡ížus̡ sn̡ím mn̡é‿t̡ažɛló ja pláč̡u]
I will-not-see him to-me sad I weep
I won't see him again. I am miserable, I keep crying…

Он так меня любил! Он так меня любил!
[ón ták m̡en̡á l̡ub̡íl ón ták m̡en̡á l̡ub̡íl]
he so me loved he so me loved
He loved me so much, he loved me so much!

36. Ни отзыва, ни слова, ни привета... 'No response, word, greeting...' Соч. 28, № 5

(A. Apukhtin) (1875)

Ни отзыва, ни слова, ни привета... Пустынею меж нами мир лежит,
[ņi ódzyva ņi slóva ņi p̧ŗiv̧ɛ́ta pustýņeju m̧ɛžnám̧i m̧ir ļɛžýt]
no response no word no greeting like-desert between-us world lies
No response, no word, no greeting... The world lies between us like a great gulf;

И мысль моя с вопросом без ответа Испуганно над сердцем тяготит!
[i mýşļ majá svaprósam b̧ɛzatv̧ɛ́ta ispúganna natşɛ́rtcɛm ţagaţít]
and thought my with-question without-answer fearfully over-heart hangs
And the unanswered question tugs painfully at my heart.

Ужель среди часов тоски и гнева Прошедшее исчезнет без следа,
[užéļ şŗeḑiç̌asóf taşķí i gņɛ́va prašɛ́tšeje‿išş̌éẓņɛt b̧ɛsşļɛdá]
really amidst-hours of-longing and rage past will-disappear without-trace
Is it possible that the past, with all those hours of longing and rage, will vanish without a trace,

Как лёгкий звук забытого напева, Как в мрак ночной упавшая звезда?
[kak ļóxkəj zvúg‿z̧abýtava nap̧ɛ́va kak vmrák naç̌nój upáfšaja z̧v̧ɛzdá]
like light sound of-forgotten refrain like into-darkness of-night falling star
Like the faint sound of a forgotten refrain, like a star falling into the void of night?

37. Страшная минута 'The terrible minute' Соч. 28, № 6

(P. Tchaikovsky) (1875)

Ты внимаешь, вниз склонив головку,
[ty v̧ņimájɛš v̧ņís sklaņív‿galófku]
you listen-closely low having-bent head
You hearken, with your dear head bent,

Очи опустив и тихо вздыхая.
[óç̌i apuşţíf‿y ţíxa vzdyxája]
eyes lowered and quietly sighing
Eyes lowered and sighing quietly.

Ты не знаешь, как мгновенья эти страшны для меня
[tý ņeznájɛš kák mgnav̧ɛ́ņja éţi strášny ḑļam̧eņá]
you do-not-know how moments these [are] terrifying for-me
You have no idea how terrifying these moments are for me,

И полны значенья, как меня смущает это молчанье.
[i pólny znač̦éņja kák m̦eņá smuș̌ș̌ájɛt ɛ́ta malč̦áņjɛ]
and full of-meaning how me embarrasses this silence
How full of portent, or how much your silences disturb me.

Я приговор твой жду, я жду решенья --
[ja p̦r̦igavór tvój ždú ja ždú r̦ɛšéņja]
I verdict your await I await decision
I await your verdict, I await your decision:

Иль нож ты мне в сердце вонзишь,
[il̦ nóš tý mņɛ́ fșɛ́rtcɛ vanz̦íš]
either knife you to-me in-heart will-thrust
Either you will plunge a knife into my heart

Иль рай мне откроешь.
[il̦ ráj mņɛ́ atkrójɛš]
or paradise to-me you-will-open
Or open a paradise before me.

Ах, не терзай меня, скажи лишь слово!
[áx ņețɛrzáj m̦eņá skažý l̦iš slóva]
ah do-not-tear at-me say only word
Ah, don't torment me! Say something, at least!

Отчего же робкое признанье
[atč̦ɛvó žɛ rópkaje‿p̦r̦izņáņjɛ]
why # shy admission
Why has my timid confession

В сердце так тебе запало глубоко?
[fșɛ́rtcɛ ták țeb̦ɛ́ zapála glubóka]
in-heart so to-you has-sunk deeply
Made such a deep impression on your heart?

Ты вздыхаешь, ты дрожишь и плачешь;
[ty vzdyxájɛš ty dražýš‿y pláč̦ɛš]
you sigh you tremble and weep
You sigh, you tremble and weep.

Иль слова любви в устах твоих немеют,
[iļ slavá ļubvi vustáx tvaíx ņemejut]
words of-love on-lips your are-mute
Do the words of love freeze on your lips,

Или ты меня жалеешь, не любишь?
[iļi tý meņá žaļéjɛš ņeļúbiš]
or you me pity not-love
Or do you pity, rather than love me?

Я приговор твой жду, я жду решенья --
[já prigavór tvój ždú ja ždú rɛšéņja]
I verdict your await I await decision
I await your verdict, I await your decision:

Иль нож ты мне в сердце вонзишь,
[iļ nóš tý mņɛ́ fsɛ́rtcɛ vanzíš]
either knife you to-me in-heart will-thrust
Either you will plunge a knife into my heart

Иль рай мне откроешь!
[iļ ráj mņɛ́ atkrójɛš]
or paradise to-me you-will-open
Or open a paradise before me.

Ах, внемли же мольбе моей,
[ax vņemļí žɛ maļbɛ́ majéj]
ah heed # entreaty my
Ah, heed my plea, please,

Отвечай, отвечай скорей!
[atveçáj atveçáj skaréj]
answer answer soon
Answer me, answer me soon!

38. Серенада Дон Жуана 'Don Juan's Serenade' Соч. 38, № 1
(A.K. Tolstoy) (1878)

Гаснут дальней Альпухары Золотистые края,
[gásnud͜dáḷṇej aḷpuxáry zalaṭístyjɛ krajá]
are-growing-dim of-distant Alpujarras golden edges
The outlines of the distant Alpujarras are growing dim.

На призывный звон гитары Выйди, милая моя!
[napṛizývnyj zvón gitáry výjḍi ṃílaja majá]
to-inviting ring of-guitar come-out darling my
Listen to the enticing message of the guitar, my darling, and come out!

Всех, кто скажет, что другая Здесь равняется с тобой,
[fṣéx kto skážɛt što drugája zḍéṣ ravṇájɛtsa stabój]
all who say that another here compares with-you
All who would say that any other woman can be compared to you,

Всех, любовию сгорая, Всех, всех зову на смертный бой!
[fṣéx ḷubóṿiju zgarája fṣéx fṣéɣ͜zavú naṣṃértnyj bój]
all with-love burning all all I-call to-mortal combat
All those burning with love, all, all I summon to mortal combat!

От лунного света Зардел небосклон;
[atlúnnava ṣṿéta zarḍél ṇɛbasklón]
from-moon's light has-reddened sky
The sky has grown red from the light of the moon.

О выйди, Нисета, Скорей на балкон!
[o výjḍi ṇiséta skaṛéj nabalkón]
oh come-out Niseta quickly onto-balcony
Oh, hurry out onto your balcony, Niseta!

От Севильи до Гренады В тихом сумраке ночей
[atṣeṿíḷji dagṛɛnády fṭíxam súmraḳɛ naĉéj]
from-Seville to-Granada in-quiet darkness of-nights
From Seville to Granada, in the quiet of the night,

Раздаются серенады, Раздаётся стук мечей.
[razdajútca ṣeṛɛnády razdajótca stúk ṃeĉéj]
resound serenades resounds clash of-sabers
Serenades resound, along with the clash of sabers.

Много крови, много песней Для прелестных льётся дам;
[mnóga króvi mnóga pésnej dlaprelésnyx ljótca dám]
much blood many songs for-lovely pours-forth ladies
Much blood and many songs pour forth for the sake of lovely ladies.

Я же той, кто всех прелестней, Всё, песнь и кровь мою отдам!
[já žɛ tój kto fséx prelésnej fsó pésn i króf majú addám]
I but to-her who of-all [is] most-lovely all song and blood my I-will-give
But I will give my blood and song, my all, to her who is loveliest of all!

39. То было раннею весной... 'It was in the early spring...' Соч. 38, № 2
(A.K. Tolstoy) (1878)

То было раннею весной, Трава едва всходила,
[tó býla ránneju vɛsnój travá jɛdvá fsxadíla]
it was in-early spring grass barely was-coming-up
It happened early in the spring. The grass was barely up,

Ручьи текли, не парил зной, И зелень рощ сквозила;
[ručjí teklí nɛpáril znóji zélen róšš skvazíla]
brooks flowed did-not-steam heat and greenery of-groves peeked-through
The brooks babbled, it was not yet sultry, and the green of the groves glistened about.

Труба пастушья по утру Ещё не пела звонко,
[trubá pastúšja pautrú ješšó nepéla zvónka]
pipe of-shepherd in-morning still not-sang ringingly
The shepherd's ringing morning song was not yet heard,

И в завитках ещё в бору Был папоротник тонкий;
[i vzavitkáx ješšó vbarú býl páparatnik tónkəj]
and in-curls still in-woods was fern slender
And in the pine-forest the delicate ferns were still in curls.

То было раннею весной, В тени берёз то было,
[tó býla ránneju vɛsnój fteni berós tó býla]
it was in-early spring in-shade of-birches it was
It happened early in the spring, in the shade of the birches it happened,

Когда с улыбкой предо мной Ты очи опустила...
[kagdá sulýpkəj predamnój tý óči apustíla]
when with-smile before-me you eyes lowered
When with a smile you lowered your eyes before me...

То на любовь мою в ответ Ты опустила вежды…
[tó naḷubóf̦ majú vatv̦ét tý apuș̦țíla v̦éždy]
then to-love my in-answer you lowered eyelids
Then in response to my love you lowered your eyes…

О жизнь! О лес! О солнца свет! О юность! О надежды!
[o žýz̦ņ o ḷés o sónca ș̦v̦ét o júnaș̦ț o nad̦éždy]
oh life oh forest oh of-sun light oh youth oh hopes
Oh, life! Oh, forest! Oh, sunshine! Oh, youth! Oh, hopes!

И плакал я перед тобой, На лик твой глядя милый.
[i plákal ja p̦er̦ettabój naḷík tvój g̦ḷád̦a m̦ílyj]
and wept I before-you on-face your gazing sweet
And I wept there in front of you, gazing into your sweet face.

То было раннею весной, В тени берёз то было!
[tó býla ráņņeju v̦esnój fțeņí b̦er̦ós tó býla]
it was in-early spring in-shade of-birches it was
It happened early in the spring, in the shade of the birches it happened,

То было утро наших лет! О счастье! О слёзы! О лес!
[tó býla útra nášyx ḷét o ș̦ș̦áș̦țjɛ o ș̦ḷózy o ḷés]
it was morning of-our years oh happiness oh tears oh forest
It was the dawn of our lives! Oh, happiness! Oh, tears! Oh, forest!

О жизнь! О солнца свет! О свежий дух берёзы!
[o žýz̦ņ o sónca ș̦v̦ét o ș̦v̦éžyj dúɣ‿b̦er̦ózy]
oh life oh of-sun light oh fresh breath of-birch
Oh, life! Oh, sunshine! Oh, fresh fragrance of birch!

40. Средь шумного бала… 'In the middle of a noisy ball…' Соч. 38, № 3
(A.K. Tolstoy) (1878)

Средь шумного бала случайно В тревоге мирской суеты
[ș̦r̦ețšúmnava bála slučájna fțr̦ɛvóg̦e‿m̦irskój sujɛtý]
amidst-noisy ball by-chance in-stress of-wordly bustle
By sheer chance, in the middle of the chaotic bustle of a noisy ball,

Тебя я увидел, но тайна Твои покрывала черты;
[ţeb̦á ja uv̦íḑɛl no tájna tvaí pakryvála č̦ɛrtý]
you I saw but secret your covered features
I caught sight of you. But some unknown secret clouded your features.

Лишь очи печально глядели, А голос так дивно звучал,
[ļiš óč̦i p̦eč̦áļna gļaḑéļi a gólas tag‿ḑívna zvuč̦ál]
only eyes sadly gazed and voice so wondrously sounded
But I noticed your eyes' sad gaze and the wondrous sound of your voice,

Как звон отдалённой свирели, Как моря играющий вал.
[kag‿zvón addaļónnəj şv̦iŗéļi kak móŗa igrájuş̦şij vál]
like ringing of-distant reed-pipe like of-sea playful surge
Like the piping of a distant flute, like a playful ocean wave.

Мне стан твой понравился тонкий И весь твой задумчивый вид,
[mņɛ́ stán tvój panráv̦ilsa tónkəj i v̦éş tvój zadúmč̦ivyj v̦ít]
to-me waist your pleased slender and all your pensive appearance
I was struck by your slender waist, by your pensive bearing.

А смех твой, и грустный и звонкий, С тех пор в моём сердце звучит.
[a şm̦ɛ́x tvój i grúsnyj i zvónkəj şţɛ́x pór vmajóm şɛ́rtcɛ zvuč̦ít]
and laugh your both melancholy and sonorous since-then in-my heart sounds
And your laugh, at once melancholy and mellifluous, still rings in my heart.

В часы одинокие ночи Люблю я, усталый, прилечь,
[fç̌asý aḑinók̦ijɛ nóč̦i ļub̦ļú ja ustályj p̦ŗiļéč̦]
in-hours lonely of-night like I tired to-lie-down
Sometimes late at night, when I am weary, I like to lie down to rest.

Я вижу печальные очи, Я слышу весёлую речь.
[ja v̦ížu p̦eč̦áļnyjɛ óč̦i ja slýšu v̦eşóluju ŗéč̦]
I see sad eyes I hear merry speech
Then I see your mournful eyes, and I hear your cheerful talk.

И грустно я, грустно так засыпаю И в грёзах неведомых сплю…
[i grúsna ja grúsna tak zasypáju i vgŗózax ņev̦édamyx şp̦ļú]
and sadly I sadly so fall-asleep and in-dreams mysterious I-sleep
And sadly then, ever so sadly, I fall asleep, only to have strange dreams…

Люблю ли тебя я не знаю,-- Но кажется мне, что люблю!
[ļuḅļu ļi ţeḅá ja ņεznáju no kážεtca mņέ što ļuḅļú]
love if you I I-do-not-know but it-seems to-me that I-love [you]
I don't know for sure whether or not I love you, but it would seem that I do.

41. О, если б ты могла... 'Oh, if only you could...' Соч. 38, № 4
(A.K. Tolstoy) (1878)

О, если б ты могла хоть на единый миг
[o jéşļip tý maglá xoţ najeḑínyj m̧ík]
oh if # you could at-least for-one moment
Oh, if only for a single moment you could

Забыть свою печаль, забыть свои невзгоды,
[zabýţ⁻ svajú ṗečáļ zabýţ⁻ svaí ņεvzgódy]
to-forget your sadness to-forget your adversities
Forget your sadness, forget your troubles.

О, если бы хоть раз я твой увидел лик,
[o jéşļi by xoţ rás ja tvój uv̧íḑεl ļík]
oh if # at-least once I your could-see face
Oh, if I could have just one glimpse of your face

Каким я знал его в счастливейшие годы!
[kaķím ja znál jεvó fşşaşļiv̧ejšyjε gódy]
such-as I knew it in-happiest years
As I knew it in the years of our bliss!

Когда в глазах твоих засветится слеза,
[kagdá vglazáx tvaíɣ‿zaşv̧éţitca şļεzá]
whenever in-eyes your glistens tear
Whenever a tear glistens in your eyes,

О, если б эта грусть могла пройти порывом,
[o jéşļi b éta grúşţ maglá prajţí parývam]
oh if # that sadness could pass like-rush
Oh, if only that grief could pass in an instant,

Как в тёплую весну пролётная гроза,
[kak fţópluju v̧εsnú praļótnaja grazá]
like in-warm spring fleeting storm
Like a fleeting thunderstorm in the warm spring-time,

Как тень от облаков, бегущая по нивам!
[kak ţéņ atablakóf ḅegúşşaja paņívam]
like shadow from-clouds running along-fields
Like the shadows from clouds racing across the fields.

42. Любовь мертвеца 'A Love from beyond the Grave' Соч. 38, № 5
(M. Lermontov) (1878)

Пускай холодною землёю засыпан я,
[puskáj xalódnaju ẓeṃḷóju zasýpan já]
although with-cold earth covered [am] I
Although I am now lying beneath the cold ground,

О друг! всегда, везде с тобою душа моя,
[o drúk f̦şɛgdá v̦eẓḍɛ́ stabój dušá majá]
oh friend always everywhere with-you soul my
Beloved! Always, everywhere my spirit is with you,

Душа моя всегда, везде с тобой!
[dušá majá f̦şɛgdá v̦eẓḍɛ́ stabój]
soul my always everywhere with-you
My spirit is with you everywhere and always!

Любви безумного томленья, жилец могил,
[ḷubv̦í ḅezúmnava taṃḷéņja žyḷɛ́c mag̦íl]
of-love mad agony denizen of-tombs
The insane agony of love I, a denizen of the tomb,

В стране покоя и забвенья я не забыл.
[fstraņɛ́ pakója i zabv̦éņja ja ņɛzabýl]
in-country of-rest and oblivion I did-not-forget
Here in the land of rest and oblivion have not forgotten.

Без страха в час последней муки покинув свет,
[ḅɛsstráxa fc̦ás paşḷéḍņej múķi paķinuf şv̦ɛ́t]
without-fear in-hour of-final torment having-forsaken world
Having fearlessly forsaken the world in the hour of my final throes,

Отрады ждал я от разлуки -- разлуки нет!
[atrády ždál ja atrazlúķi razlúķi ņét]
comfort awaited I from-separation separation there-is-not
I anticipated consolation in separation from you--but there is no separation!

Что мне сиянье божьей власти и рай святой!
[štó mņέ şijáņjε bóžjej vlá şţi i ráj şyatój]
what to-me [is] radiance of-God's kingdom and paradise holy
What are God's glorious kingdom and holy paradise to me!

Я перенёс земные страсти туда с собой.
[ja peŗeņóz‿ẓεmnýjε strá şţi tudá ssabój]
I conveyed earthly passions there with-me
I have taken all my earthly passions there with me.

Ласкаю я мечту родную везде одну;
[laskáju já mečtú radnúju yeẓdέ adnú]
cherish I dream beloved everywhere same
Everywhere I cherish the same beloved dream,

Желаю, плачу и ревную, как в старину.
[žεláju pláçu i ŗεvnúju kak fstaŗinú]
I-desire weep and am-jealous as long-ago
I feel the same desire, pain, and jealousy as long ago.

Коснётся ль чуждое дыханье твоих ланит, --
[kaşņótca ļ çúždajε dyxáņjε tvaíx laņít]
will-touch # another's breath your cheeks
Should someone else's breath touch your cheeks--

Моя душа в немом страданьи вся задрожит;
[majá dušá vņεmóm stradáņji fşá zadražýt]
my soul in-mute suffering all will-shudder
Then my soul in silent suffering would begin to shudder.

Случится ль, шепчешь, засыпая, ты о другом --
[slučítca ļ šέpçεž‿zasypája ty adrugóm]
will-happen # whisper falling-asleep you about-another
If you should ever whisper about someone else as you fall asleep,

Твои слова текут, пылая по мне огнём!
[tvaí slavá ţεkút pylája pamņέ agņóm]
your words flow flaming over-me like-fire
Your words would flow over me, searing me like fire.

43. Флорентинская песня* 'Florentine Song' Соч. 38, № 6
Pimpinella
(Translated from the Italian by P. Tchaikovsky) (1878)

Если ты хочешь, желанная, знать, что я в сердце таю, --
[jéşļi ty xóçɛž‿žɛlánnaja znáţ štó ja fşɛ́rtcɛ tajú]
if you want sweetheart to-know what I in-heart keep-secret
If you want to know, sweetheart, what secret I harbor in my heart:

Ревность какая-то странная душу терзает мою!
[ŗɛ́vnaşţ kakájata stránnaja dúšu ţɛrzájɛt majú]
jealousy some-sort-of strange soul tears my
A strange feeling of jealousy keeps searing in my soul.

Чары, тебе Богом данные, лишь для меня расточай,
[çáry ţeþɛ́ bógam dánnyjɛ ļíž‿dļaṃeņá rastaçáj]
charms to-you by-God given only for-me lavish
Lavish your God-given charms only on me

И на признанья нежданные гневно, мой друг, отвечай!
[i naprıznáņja ņɛždánnyjɛ gņɛ́vna mój drúk atveçáj]
and to-declarations unexpected angrily my dear reply
And reply indignantly to overtures from anyone else.

Я молю тебя: и взглядом и улыбкой радуй меня одного.
[ja maļú ţeþá i vzgļádam i ulýpkəj ráduj ṃeņá adnavó]
I beg you both by-glance and by-smile delight me alone
I implore you: gladden only me with your gaze and your smile.

Очи твои так светлы, так прекрасны, краше здесь нет лица;
[óçi tvaí tak şvɛ́tly tak pŗɛkrásny kráše zdɛ́ş ņɛ́t ļicá]
eyes your so bright so lovely more-beautiful here there-is-no face
Your eyes are so bright and lovely. There is no face hereabout lovelier than yours.

Речи твои пленительны, опасны, губишь ты все сердца! Ах!
[ŗɛ́çi tvaí pļeņíţeļny apásny gúþiš ty fşé şɛrtcá áx]
words your [are] captivating dangerous destroy you all hearts ah
Your words are captivating and dangerous, destroying everyone's heart. Ah!

---

*This text is a translation of an Italian original. The song is often sung in Italian.

Будь же довольна, желанная, сердцем покорным одним;
[búḑ‿žɛ davóḷna žɛlánnaja şértcɛm pakórnym adņím]
be # content darling with-heart submissive one
Please be content with just one obedient heart, my darling.

Чтоб не страдал непрестанно я, будь недоступна другим!
[štob ņɛstradál ņep̧ŗɛstánna já búţ ņɛdastúpna druģím]
so-that not-suffer constantly I be inaccessible to-others
Remain distant from all others, so that I don't have to suffer endlessly.

Ах, одного меня, радуй меня одного, лишь одного меня,
[áx adnavó m̧eņá ráduj m̧eņá adnavó ḷíš adnavó m̧eņá]
ah alone me gladden me alone only alone me
Ah, me alone, gladden only me alone, only me,

Милый друг мой, лишь одного меня!
[m̧ílyj drúk mój ḷíš adnavó m̧eņá]
dear friend my only alone me
Me, me alone, my darling!

44. Кабы знала я...* **'If I had known...'** Соч. 47, № 1
(A.K. Tolstoy) (1880)

Кабы знала я, кабы ведала, Не смотрела бы из окошечка
[káby znála já káby ỵédala ņɛsmaţŗéla by izakóšɛç̌ka]
if knew I if been-aware not-looked would out-of-window
If only I had known, had been aware, I wouldn't have looked out the window

Я на молодца разудалого, Как он ехал по нашей улице,
[ja namólatca razudálava kak on jéxal panášej úḷicɛ]
I at-youth dashing as he rode down-our street
At the dashing young hunter riding down our street,

Набекрень заломивши мурмолку, Как лихого коня буланого,
[nab̧eķŗéņ zalam̧ífšy múrmalku kak ḷixóva kaņá bulánava]
aslant having-cocked cap like bold steed dun
With his cap cocked to one side, as his bold dun stallion,

---

*This text is in folk dialect. The speaker of this text is a woman.

Звонконогого, долгогривого,   Супротив окон на дыбы вздымал!
[zvankanógava   dalgag̦ŗ́ivava   supraţ́ifakón   nadybý   vzdymál]
ringing-hoofed   long-maned   across-from-windows on-hind-legs reared
With its ringing hoofs and long mane, he made rear up on its back legs!

Кабы знала я, кабы ведала,   Для него бы я не рядилася,
[káby znála já káby v̦ɛ́dala   d̦l̦an̦ɛvó by   já   n̦eŗad̦́ilasa]
if   knew   I   if   been-aware for-him   would I   not-got-dressed-up
If only I had known, had been aware, I would not have donned my best for him,

С золотой каймой ленту алую   В косу динную не вплетала бы,
[zzalatój   kajmój   l̦ɛ́ntu   áluju   fkósu   d̦ĺ̦innuju n̦ef̦p̦l̦ɛtála   by]
with-golden fringe   ribbon   scarlet   into-braid long   not-have-braided   would
Would not have woven into my long braid the scarlet ribbon with the golden fringe,

Рано до свету не вставала бы,   За околицу не спешила бы,
[rána dóșv̦ɛtu   n̦ɛfstavála by   zaakól̦icu   n̦eșp̦ɛšýla   by]
early   before-light not-got-up   would beyond-village-edge not-have-hurried would
Would not have arisen before dawn, would not have rushed out of the village,

В росе ноженьки не мочила бы,   На просёлок тот не глядела бы,--
[vrașɛ́ nóžen̦k̦i n̦ɛmač̦́ila by   naprașólak tót   n̦egl̦ad̦ɛ́la   by]
in-dew feet   not-got-wet would at-road   that not-have-watched would
Would not have wet my feet in the dew, would not have gazed down that country road,

Не проедет ли тем просёлком он,   На руке держа пёстра сокола?
[n̦ɛprajéd̦ɛt   l̦i   ţ́ɛm   prașólkam   ón naruk̦é d̦ɛržá   p̦óstra sókala]
will-not-pass-by #   on-that road   he   on-hand   holding   colorful   falcon
In case he should pass by on it, holding a bright-colored falcon on his hand.

Кабы знала я, кабы ведала,   Не сидела бы поздним вечером
[káby znála já   káby v̦ɛ́dala   n̦eșid̦ɛ́la   by   póz̦n̦im   v̦ɛ́č̦ɛram]
if   knew   I   if   been-aware   not-have-sat would in-late   evening
If only I had known, had been aware, I would not have sat there late in the evening,

Пригорюнившись на завалине,   На завалине близ колодезя,
[p̦ŗigaŗún̦ifšyș   nazavál̦in̦ɛ   nazavál̦in̦e   b̦l̦iskalód̦ez̦a]
having-grown-sad on-mound-of-earth   on-mound-of-earth   near-well
Dejected, on that earth-mound, on the mound near the well,

Поджидаючи да гадаючи, Не придёт ли он, ненаглядный мой!
[padžydájuçi da gadájuči ņepŗiḑót ļi ón ņenagļádnyj mój]
anxiously-waiting and guessing will-not-come whether he beloved my
Waiting anxiously and wondering whether or not my beloved would come.

Ах! Не придёт ли он, ненаглядный мой,
[áx ņepŗiḑót ļi ón ņɛnagļádnyj mój]
ah will-not-come whether he beloved my
Ah! Whether or not my beloved would come

Напоить коня студеной водой!
[napaíţ kaņá stuḑɛnój vadój]
to-water horse with-cold water
To water his horse with the cold water.

Кабы знала я, кабы ведала. Ах!
[káby znála já káby ү̦ɛ́dala áx]
if knew I if been-aware ah
If only I had known, had been aware. Ah!

45. Горними тихо летела душа небесами... Соч. 47, № 2
'A soul flew quietly through the lofty heavens...'
(A. K. Tolstoy) (1880)

Горними тихо летела душа небесами,
[górņimi ţíxa ļeţɛ́la dušá ņeb̦ɛsáṃi]
through-lofty quietly flew soul heavens
A soul was flying silently through the heavenly heights.

Грустные долу она опускала ресницы;
[grúsnyjɛ dólu aná apuskála ŗeşņícy]
sad down she lowered eyelashes
Sadly she closed her eyes.

Слёзы, в пространство от них упадая звездами,
[şļózy fprastránstva atņíx upadája ẓү̦ɛzdáṃi]
tears into-space from-them falling as-stars
Tears falling from them into space as stars

Светлой и длинной вилися за ней вереницей.
[şv̧ɛ́tləj i ḑļínnəj v̧iļisa zaņéj v̧eŗeņícej]
like-bright and long whirled after-her string
Whirled along behind her in a bright long string.

Встречные тихо её вопрошали светила:
[f̧şţŗéç̌nyje‿ţíxa jejó vaprašáļi şv̧eţíla]
oncoming quietly her questioned heavenly-bodies
Oncoming luminaries asked her quietly:

«Что ты грустна? И о чём эти слёзы во взоре?»
[štó tý grusná i aç̌óm éţi şļózy vavzóŗɛ]
why you [are] sad and about-what these tears in-eyes
"Why are you sad? And why are you shedding tears?"

Им отвечала она: «Я земли не забыла,
[ím atv̧eç̌ála aná ja z̧em̧ļí ņɛzabýla]
to-them answered she I earth have-not-forgotten
She replied: "I have not forgotten the earth.

Много оставила там я страданья и горя.
[mnóga astáv̧ila tám ja stradáņja i góŗa]
much left-behind there I suffering and woe
I left much suffering and tribulation behind me there.

Здесь я лишь ликом блаженства и радости внемлю,
[z̧ḑéş ja ļiš ļikam blažɛ́nstva i rádaşţi v̧ņém̧ļu]
here I only with-face bliss and joy perceive
Here I only give the appearance of sharing in the the bliss and joy.

Праведных души не знают ни скорби ни злобы,--
[práv̧ɛdnyɣ‿dúšy ņɛznájut ņi skórb̧i ņi zlóby]
of-righteous souls not-know neither grief nor malice
The souls of the righteous know nothing either of grief or malice.

О, отпусти меня снова, Создатель, на землю,
[o atpuşţí m̧eņá snóva sazdáţeļ naz̧ém̧ļu]
oh release me again Creator to-earth
Oh, Creator, let me return to the earth!

Было б о ком пожалеть и утешить кого бы!»
[býla b akóm pažaļéţ i uţéšyţ kavó by]
be would about-whom to-pity and to-console whom #
There would be many there I could pity and console!"

46. На землю сумрак пал...* 'Dusk has covered the earth...' Соч. 47, № 3
(N. Berg, after Mickiewicz) (1880)

На землю сумрак пал; не шелохнут кусты;
[nazémļu súmrak pál ņešelaxnút kustý]
onto-earth dusk fell not-stir bushes
Dusk has covered the earth. The bushes are completely still.

Свернулись лилии поблекшие листы,
[şyernúļiş ļiļii pabļékšyje‿listý]
have-curled-up of-lily faded leaves
The lily's faded leaves have curled up tightly

И тихо озеро почило.
[i ţíxa ózera pačíla]
and quietly lake has-gone-to-sleep
And quietly the lake has gone to sleep.

Под обаянием волшебной красоты,
[padabajáņijem valšébnəj krasatý]
under-charm of-magical beauty
Under the spell of this magical beauty

Стою, задумавшись. «Что грустен нынче ты,
[stajú zadúmafšyş štó grúşţen nýnče tý]
I-stand having-grown-pensive why sad now you
I stand, deep in thought. "Why are you sorrowful now

И всё кругом тебя уныло?»
[i fşó krugóm ţeþá unýla]
and all around you mournful
And why does everything around you seem sad?"

*The speaker of this text is a woman.

Поутру прихожу, оживлена росой,
[paútru p̧ŗixažú ažyvļená rasój]
in-morning I-come invigorated by-dew
In the morning I come here, refreshed by the dew,

Проснулась лилия, блистая красотой,
[prasnúlaş ļíļija b̧ļistája krasatój]
has-awakened ily shining in-beauty
And the lily now has awakened, radiant in its beauty,

И, милая, в блистающей одежде,
[i m̧ílaja vb̧ļistájuşşej aḑéžḑɛ]
and dear-one in-shining clothes
And, dear sweet thing, in its glistening attire,

С улыбкою привет на небо шлёт она,
[sulýpkaju p̧ŗiv̧ét naņéba šļót aná]
with-smile greeting to-sky sends she
Sends heavenward a smiling greeting,

И плещет в озере весёлая волна…
[i p̧ļéşşɛt vózeŗe‿v̧eşólaja valná]
and splashes in-lake merry wave
While waves splash merrily in the lake…

А я? Мне грустно, как и прежде!
[a já mņé grúsna kák‿y p̧ŗéžḑɛ]
and I to-me sad as also formerly
And I? I am just as sad as before.

47. Усни, печальный друг… 'Go to sleep, sad friend…' Соч. 47, № 4
(A.K. Tolstoy) (1880)

Усни, печальный друг, уже с грядущей тьмой
[uşņí p̧eçáļnyj drúk užé zgŗadúşşej ţmój]
go-to-sleep sad friend already with-approaching darkness
Go to sleep, my sad friend. Already oncoming darkness

Вечерний алый свет сливается всё боле,
[v̦eč̦ɛ́rn̦ij ályj șv̦ɛ́t șl̦ivájɛtsa f̦șó ból̦ɛ]
evening's scarlet color is-fusing more-and more
Is overtaking twilight's rosey hue.

Блеящие стада вернулися домой,
[b̦l̦ejáș̌ș̌ijɛ stadá v̦ɛrnúl̦isa damój]
bleating flocks have-returned home
Bleating flocks have made their way home

И улеглася пыль на опустелом поле.
[i ul̦ɛglása pýl̦ naapușțɛ́lam pól̦ɛ]
and settled dust on-emptied field
And the dust has settled on the deserted fields.

Да снидет ангел сна, прекрасен и крылат,
[da șn̦íd̦ɛt áng̦ɛl sná p̦r̦ɛkráșɛn‿y krylát]
may descend angel of-sleep lovely and winged
May the sweet winged angel of sleep descend to you

И да перенесёт тебя он в жизнь иную!
[i da p̦ɛr̦ɛn̦ɛșót țɛb̦á ón vžýz̦n̦ inúju]
and may transport you he to-life another
And bear you off to another world.

Издавна был он мне в печали друг и брат,
[izdávna býl ón mn̦ɛ́ fp̦ɛč̦ál̦i drúk‿y brát]
long-since was he to-me in-sadness friend and brother
Long has he been a friend and brother to me in times of sadness.

Усни, моё дитя, к нему я не ревную.
[ușn̦í majó d̦ițá kn̦ɛmú ja n̦ɛr̦ɛvnúju]
go-to-sleep my child of-him I am-not-jealous
Go to sleep, my child, I feel no jealousy toward him.

На раны сердца он забвение прольёт,
[narány șɛ́rtca ón zabv̦ɛ́n̦ijɛ pral̦jót]
on-wounds of-heart he oblivion will-pour
He will pour forgetfulness onto the wounds of your heart,

Пытливую тоску от разума отнимет
[pytl̡ívuju taskú atrázuma atn̡ím̡ɛt]
probing anguish from-mind will-remove
Remove probing anguish from your mind,

И с горестной души на ней лежащий гнёт
[i zgór̡ɛsnəj dušý nan̡éj l̡ɛžáš̡š̡ij gn̡ót]
and from-sorrowing soul on-it lying weight
And the heavy weight that oppresses your sorrowing soul

До нового утра незримо приподнимет.
[danóvava utrá n̡ez̡r̡íma p̡r̡ipadn̡ím̡ɛt]
before-new morning invisibly will-lift
By tomorrow's sunrise he will invisibly raise.

Томимая весь день душевною борьбой,
[tam̡ímaja v̡éz̡‿d̡én̡ dušɛ́vnaju bar̡bój]
tormented all day by-spiritual struggle
Tormented all day long by your spiritual struggle,

От взоров и речей враждебных ты устала;
[advzóraf i r̡eč̡éj vraž̡d̡ɛ́bnyx tý ustála]
from-looks and comments hostile you have-grown-tired
You have grown weary from hostile looks and utterances.

Усни, моё дитя, меж ними и тобой
[us̡n̡í majó d̡it̡á m̡ɛžn̡ím̡i i tabój]
go-to-sleep my child between-them and you
Go to sleep, my child. Between them and you

Он благостной рукой опустит покрывало.
[ón blágasnəj rukój apús̡t̡it pakryvála]
he with-kind hand will-lower cover
He will lower a protective curtain with his kind hand.

Усни, моё дитя!
[us̡n̡í majó d̡it̡á]
go-to-sleep my child
Go to sleep, my child!

48. Благословляю вас, леса... 'The Song of the Pilgrim' Соч. 47, № 5
(A.K. Tolstoy) (1880)

Благословляю вас, леса, Долины, нивы, горы, воды,
[blagaslaʋ̦l̦áju vás l̦ɛsá dal̦íny n̦ívy góry vódy]
I-bless you forests vales fields mountains waters
I bless you , forests, vales, fields, mountains, waters.

Благословляю я свободу И голубые небеса!
[blagaslaʋ̦l̦áju já svabódu i galubýje‿n̦eb̦ɛsá]
bless I liberty and blue skies
I bless liberty and heaven's blue skies.

И посох мой благословляю, И эту бедную суму,
[i pósax mój blagaslaʋ̦l̦áju i ɛ́tu b̦ɛ́dnuju sumú]
and staff my I-bless and this poor bag
I bless even this my staff and this my humble traveler's pouch,

И степь от краю и до краю, И солнца свет, и ночи тьму,
[i ș̦țɛ́p̦ atkráju i dakráju i sónca ș̦ʋ̦ɛ́t i nóç̦i țmú]
and steppe from-edge and to-edge and of-sun light and of-night darkness
And the steppe, from horizon to horizon, and the light of the sun, and the dark of the night;

И одинокую тропинку, По коей, нищий, я иду,
[i ad̦inókuju trap̦ínku pakójej n̦íș̦ș̦ij ja idú]
and lonely path along-which beggar I walk
And this lonely path along which I, a mendicant, walk;

И в поле каждую былинку, И в небе каждую звезду!
[i fpól̦ɛ kážduju byl̦ínku i vn̦éb̦ɛ kážduju z̦ʋ̦ɛzdú]
and in-field every blade-of-grass and in-sky every star
And every blade of grass in the field, and every star in the sky!

О, если б мог всю жизнь смешать я, Всю душу вместе с вами слить!
[o jéș̦l̦i b mók f̦ș̦ú žýz̦n̦ ș̦m̦ɛšáț ja f̦ș̦ú dúšu ʋ̦m̦éș̦țɛ svám̦i ș̦l̦íț]
oh if # could whole life to-combine I whole soul together with-you to-fuse
Oh, if only I could combine my whole life with you all, fuse my entire soul with you!

О, если б мог в мои объятья Я вас, враги, друзья и братья,
[o jéș̦l̦i b mók vmaí abjáțja ja vás vrag̦i druz̦já i bráțja]
oh if # could into-my embraces I you foes friends and brothers
Oh, if only I could fit into my embrace all of you, my foes, my friends, my brothers,

И всю природу в мои объятья Заключить!
[i fşú p̧ŗiródu vmaí abjáţja zak̦ļuç̌íţ]
and all nature into-my embraces include
And all of nature encompass in my embrace!

49. День ли царит... 'Is it day, or night?...' Соч. 47, № 6
(A. Apukhtin) (1880

День ли царит, тишина ли ночная,
[ḑéņ ļi caŗít ţišyná ļi naç̌nája]
does-day # reign silence or nocturnal
Is it now daytime or nighttime?

В снах ли бессвязных, в житейской борьбе,--
[fsnáx ļi b̧ɛşşy̧áznyx vžyţéjskəj baŗb̧ɛ́]
in-dreams # disjointed in-everyday struggle
Whether in my chaotic dreams, or in my grapplings with everyday life,

Всюду со мной, мою жизнь наполняя,
[f̧şúdu samnój majú žýz̧ņ napalņája]
everywhere with-me my life filling
Everywhere I go, filling my very being,

Дума всё та же одна роковая,-- Всё о тебе!
[dúma f̧şó tá žɛ adná rakavája f̧şó aţeb̧ɛ́]
thought keeps one and same fateful always about you
There keeps recurring one and the same fateful thought--about you, always about you.

С нею не страшен мне призрак былого,
[sņéju ņɛstrášɛn mņe‿p̧ŗízrag‿bylóva]
with-it not-terrifying to-me phantom of-past
Armed with this thought, the specter of the past is not frightening.

Сердце воспрянуло снова любя...
[şɛ́rtcɛ vaşp̧ŗánula snóva ļub̧á]
heart is-revived again loving
My heart awakens in renewed love...

Вера, мечты, вдохновенное слово,--
[v̦éra m̦eč̦tý vdaxnav̦ɛ́nnajɛ slóva]
faith dreams inspired word
My faith, my dreams, my inspiration,

Всё, что в душе дорогого, святого,-- Всё от тебя!
[f̦șó što vdušɛ́ daragóva șv̦atóva f̦șó ațțeb̦á
all that in-soul [is] dear holy all from you
All that is dear and sacred in my soul comes from you--all from you!

Будут ли дни мои ясны, унылы,
[búdut l̦i d̦n̦í maí jásny unýly]
be if days my bright sad
Whether my days be bright or cheerless,

Скоро ли сгину я, жизнь загубя,--
[skóra l̦i z̦g̦ínu ja žýz̦n̦ zagub̦á]
soon if vanish I life destroying
Whether I soon vanish, my life destroyed--

Знаю одно, что до самой могилы
[znáju adnó što dasáməj mag̦íly]
I-know one-thing that to-very tomb
I know one thing: that until I am in my tomb

Помыслы, чувства и песни, и силы,-- Всё для тебя!
[pómysly č̦ústva i p̦éșn̦i i șíly f̦șó d̦l̦ațeb̦á]
thoughts feelings and songs and powers all for-you
All my plans, yearnings, successes, and prospects--all are for you!

50. Я ли в поле да не травушка была...* — Соч. 47, № 7
'Was I not like grass in the field?...'

(I. Surikov) (1880)

Я ли в поле да не травушка была, Я ли в поле не зелёная росла;
[já l̦i fpól̦ɛ da n̦ɛ trávuška bylá já l̦i fpól̦e‿n̦e‿z̦el̦ónaja raslá]
I # in-field # not grass was I # in-field not green grew
Was I not like grass in the field, was I not like green grass growing in the field?

*This text is in folk dialect. The speaker of this text is a woman.

Взяли меня, травушку, скосили, На солнышке в поле иссушили.
[vzáli meñá trávušku skasíli nasólnyškɛ fpólɛ issušýli]
they-took me grass they-mowed in-sun in-field [me] they-dried
They took me, like grass, and mowed me down and dried me out in the sun.

Ох, ты, горе моё, горюшко! Знать, знать такая моя долюшка!
[óx tý górɛ majó góruška znát znát takája majá dóluška]
oh you woe my bitter-woe clearly clearly such [is] my fate
Oh, woe is me, bitter woe! Such is my fate, it seems!

Я ли в поле не калинушка была, Я ли в поле да не красная росла;
[já li fpólɛ‿ɲɛ kalínuška bylá já li fpólɛ da ɲɛ krásnaja raslá]
I # in-field not snowball-tree was I # in-field # not beautiful grew
Was I not like a snowball-tree in the field? Was I not beautiful as I grew?

Взяли калинушку, сломали Да в жгутики меня посвязали!
[vzáli kalínušku slamáli da vžgútiki meñá pasvazáli]
they-took snowball-tree they-broke and into bundles me tied
They took me, like a snowball-tree, and broke me and tied me up in bundles.

Я ль у батюшки не доченька была, У родимой не цветочек я росла;
[já l ubátuški ɲɛ dóčeɲka bylá uradímәj ɲɛ cvɛtóčɛk ja raslá]
I # by-papa not dear-daughter was by-mama not little-flower I grew
Was I not my father's beloved daughter? Was I not my mother's little flower as I grew up?

Неволей меня, бедную, взяли, Да с немилым, седым повенчали!
[ɲɛvólej meñá bédnuju vzáli da sɲemílym sedým pavenčáli]
not-by-will me poor-one they-took and with-unloved gray-haired married
Against my will they took wretched me and forced me to marry an old man I do not love.

51. Бабушка и внучек 'Grandmother and Grandson' Соч. 54, № 1
(A. Pleshcheev) (1883)

Под окном чулок старушка Вяжет в комнате уютной
[padaknóm čulók starúška vážɛt fkómnatɛ ujútnәj]
under-window sock old-woman knits in-room cozy
In a cozy room under a window sits an old woman knitting a sock.

И в очки свои большие Смотрит в угол поминутно.
[i vačkí svaí balšýjɛ smótrit vúgal paminútna]
and through-glasses her large looks into-corner every-minute
Every minute or so she looks through her large spectacles into the corner.

А в углу кудрявый мальчик молча К стенке прислонился.
[a vuglú kuḑŗávyj mál̦ç̦ik mólç̦a kş̦ţɛ́nķe_p̧ŗislaņílsa]
and in-corner curly-headed boy silently against-wall has-leaned
In the corner a curly-haired boy leans silently against the wall.

На лице его забота, Взгляд на что-то устремился.
[naļicé_jɛvó zabóta vzgļát naštóta uş̦ţŗem̧ílsa]
on-face his worry gaze onto-something fixed
There is concern on his face as he stares intently at something.

«Что сидишь всё дома, внучек? Шёл бы в сад, копал бы грядки
[što şiḑíš f̧şó dóma vnúç̦ɛk šól by fsát kapál by gŗátķi]
why sit-you all-time home grandson you-go should into-garden dig should patches
"Why do you sit around the house, grandson? You should go into the garden and dig some vegetable patches.

Или кликнул бы сестрёнку, Поиграл бы с ней в лошадки».
[iļi ķļíknul by şeş̦ţŗónku paigrál by sņéj vlašátķi]
or call should sister play-awhile should with-her at-horses
Or maybe call your sister and play at horses with her awhile.

Подошёл к старушке внучек И головкою курчавой
[padašól kstarúšķɛ vnúç̦ɛk i galófkaju kurç̦ávəj]
approached to-old-woman grandson and head curly
Up to the old woman walks the boy, and his curly head

К ней припал. Он молчит, глаза большие На неё глядят лукаво…
[kņéj p̧ŗipál ón malç̦íḑ_glazá baļšýjɛ naņejó gļaḑát lukáva]
to-her pressed he is-silent eyes big at-her gaze slyly
He presses against her. He is silent, but his eyes gaze at her slyly.

«Знать, гостинцу захотелось? -- Говорит ему старушка,--
[znáḑ_gaş̦ţíncu zaxaţélaş gavaŗít jɛmú starúška]
it-seems some-sweets you-would-like says to-him old-woman
"I suppose you'd like some sweets?" says the old woman to him,

Винных ягод, винограду, Иль тебе нужна игрушка?»
[v̧ínnyx jágat v̧inagrádu iļ ţeb̧ɛ́ nužná igrúška]
some-figs # some-grapes or to-you [is] needed toy
"Or some figs or grapes? Or do you want a toy?"

«Нет, гостинцев мне не надо! У меня игрушек много.
[ṇέd‿gaṣṭincεf mṇέ‿ṇεnáda umẹṇá igrúšεk mnóga]
no figs to-me not-needed I-have of-toys plenty
"No, I don't want any figs! And I have plenty of toys.

Сумку ты купи Да в школу покажи-ка мне дорогу».
[súmku tý kuṗí da fškólu pakažýka mṇέ darógu]
schoolbag you buy and to-school show me way
Just buy me a schoolbag and show me the way to the schoolhouse.

52. Птичка 'The Little Bird'

Соч. 54, № 2

(A. Pleshcheev)

(1883)

Птичка божия проснулася с зарёю,
[ṗṭíčka bóžyja prasnúlasa zzaṛóju]
bird of-God awoke with-dawn
A bird in the service of God awoke with the dawn

А уж пахаря застала за сохою.
[a uš páxaṛa zastála zasaxóju]
and already plowman found at-plow
To find the plowman already at work with his plow.

Полетит она к лазурным небесам
[paḷeṭít aná klazúrnym ṇeḅεsám]
will-fly it to-azure heavens
Off it flies to the azure heavens,

И, что видит в сёлах, всё расскажет там.
[i štó ṿíḍit fṣólax fṣó rasskážεt tám]
and what sees in-villages all will-tell there
To relate there all that it sees in the villages below.

Скажет птичка Богу, что бедняк страдает,
[skážεt ṗṭíčka bógu što ḅeḍṇák stradájεt]
will-say bird to-God that poor-man suffers
The bird tells God how much the poor peasant suffers,

Что кровавым потом ниву орошает.
[što kravávym pótam ṇívu arašájεt]
that by-bloody sweat field irrigates
How he waters his fields with his own sweat and blood.

Не мила, как птичке, пахарю весна:
[n̡em̡ilá kak p̡t̡íč̡k̡ɛ páxar̡u v̡ɛsná]
not-beloved as to-bird to-plowman spring
Spring is not as dear to the plowman as it is to the bird.

Не несёт с собою радостей она…
[n̡en̡es̡ót ssabóju rádas̡t̡ej aná]
not-bears with-it joys it
It brings him no joy.

Встретил бы он солнце песенкой весёлой,
[fs̡t̡r̡ét̡il by ón sónce‿p̡és̡ɛnkəj v̡es̡óləj]
meet would he sun with-song merry
He would like to greet the morning sun with a cheerful song,

Да молчать заставит гнёт нужды тяжёлый.
[da malč̡ád̡‿zastáv̡id‿gn̡ót nuždý t̡ažóləj]
but to-be-silent will-force weight of-need heavy
But the weight of dire need prevents such singing.

На сердце заботы, как свинец, лежат,
[nás̡ɛrtcɛ zabóty kak s̡v̡in̡ɛ́c l̡ɛžát]
on-heart worries like lead lie
Cares lie heavily on his heart, like lead.

Поневоле песня не пойдёт на лад.
[pan̡ɛvól̡e‿p̡és̡n̡a n̡epajd̡ót nalát]
against-will song will-not-go to-harmony
A forced song cannot ring true.

Скажет птичка Богу, чтоб его рука
[skážɛt p̡t̡íč̡ka bógu štob jɛvó ruká]
will-say bird to-God that His hand
The bird tells God that He should with His hand

Поддержала в горькой доле бедняка.
[padd̡ɛržála vgór̡kəj dól̡e‿b̡ed̡n̡aká]
support in-bitter lot poor-man
Support the poor peasant in his bitter fate,

Чтоб ему нести свой крест достало силы,
[štob jɛmú ņeşţí svój ķŗɛ́zd‿dastála şíly]
so-that to-him to-bear his cross suffice strength
So that he might have the strength to bear his cross,

Чтоб без ропота добрёл он до могилы...
[štob ḅɛzrópata daḅŗól ón damag̡íly]
so-that without-grumbling reach he to-grave
So that he might make his way to the tomb without complaint.

53. Весна 'Spring'

(A. Pleshcheev)

Соч. 54, № 3
(1883)

Травка зеленеет, солнышко блестит, Ласточка с весною в сени к нам летит.
[tráfka ẓeļeņéjɛt sólnyška ḅļeşţít lástaçka sɣɛsnóju fşéņi kná m ļeţít]
grass is-green sun shines swallow with-spring into-porch to-us flies
The grass is green, the sun is shining. The spring brings the swallow, flying onto our porch.

С нею солнце ярче и весна милей...
[sņéju sónce‿járçɛ i ɣɛsná ṃiļéj]
with-it sun [is] brighter and spring [is] dearer
It makes the sun seem brighter and the spring sweeter.

Прощебечь с дороги нам привет скорей.
[praşşeḅéḑẓ‿ẓdaróg̡i nám ṗŗiɣét skaŗéj]
chirp from-road to-us greeting quickly
Sing us a song from the road here, hurry!

Дам тебе я зёрен, а ты песню спой,
[dám ţeḅé‿ja ẓóŗɛn a tý ṗéşņu spój]
will-give to-you some-grain and you song sing
I'll give you some grain if you'll sing us a song

Что из стран далёких принесла с собой...
[štó isstrán daļóķix ṗŗiņɛslá ssabój]
which from-countries distant brought with-you
From the distant lands you have visited.

54. Мой садик 'My Little Garden' Соч. 54, №4
(A. Pleshcheev) (1883)

Как мой садик свеж и зелен! Распустилась в нём сирень;
[kák mój sádik şy̧έš‿y z̧él̡ɛn raspuştílaş vn̡óm şirén̡]
how my garden [is] fresh and green has-bloomed in-it lilacs
How fresh and green my garden is! The lilacs there are in full bloom.

От черёмухи душистой И от лип кудрявых тень...
[atç̡eŗómux̡i dušýstəj i atl̡íp kud̡rávyx t̡én̡]
from-bird-cherry-tree fragrant and from-lindens curly-leafed shade
There is shade from the fragrant bird-cherry tree and the curly-leafed lindens.

Правда, нет в нём бледных лилий, Горделивых георгин,
[právda n̡έt vn̡óm b̡l̡έdnyx l̡íl̡ij gard̡el̡ívyɣ‿g̡ɛarg̡ín]
true is-not in-it pale lilies proud dahlias
True, there are no pale lilies there, or proud dahlias,

И лишь пёстрые головки Возвышает мак один.
[i l̡iš p̡óstryjɛ galófk̡i vazvyšájɛt mák ad̡ín]
and only colorful heads raises poppy alone
There only poppies raise high their colorful heads.

Да подсолнечник у входа, Словно верный часовой,
[da patsóln̡eç̡n̡ik ufxóda slóvna v̡έrnyj ç̡asavój]
and sunflower by-entrance like faithful sentry
And the sunflower at the gate, like a faithful sentry,

Сторожит себе дорожку, Всю поросшую травой...
[staražýt şeb̡έ daróšku fş̡ú paróššuju travój]
guards his path all overgrwon with-grass
Watches over the pathway all overgrown with grass.

Но люблю я садик скромный: Он душе моей милей
[no l̡ub̡l̡ú ja sád̡ik skrómnyj ón dušέ majéj m̡il̡éj]
but love I garden modest it to-soul my dearer
But I love my modest garden. It is dearer to my heart

Городских садов унылых, С сетью правильных аллей.
[garatşk̡íx sadóf unýlyx şşétju práv̡il̡nyx al̡éj]
than-urban gardens melancholy with-network of-regular alleys
Than melancholy urban gardens, with their networks of orderly rows.

И весь день в траве высокой, Лёжа, слушать бы я рад,
[i ʋéz͜ ḍéṇ ftraʋɛ́ vysókəj ḷóža slúšaḍ͜ by ja rát]
and all day in-grass tall lying to-listen would-be I glad
And all day long I would gladly lie in the tall grass, listening

Как заботливые пчёлы Вкруг черёмухи жужжат.
[kág͜ zabótḷivyje͜ p̣çóly fkrukčeṛómuxi žuẓẓát]
how industrious bees around-bird-cherry-tree buzz
To the industrious bees buzzing around the bird-cherry tree.

55. Легенда 'A Legend'

(A. Pleshcheev)

Соч. 54, № 5
(1883)

Был у Христа-младенца сад, и много роз взрастил он в нём.
[býl uxṛistá mlaḍénca sát i mnóga róz͜ vzraṣṭíl on vṇóm]
was by-Christ youngster garden and many roses raised He in-it
When Christ was still a boy he had a garden in which many roses grew.

Он трижды в день их поливал, чтоб сплесть венок себе потом.
[ón ṭṛiždy vḍéṇ íx paḷivál štob ṣp̣ḷéṣṭ ʋɛnók ṣeb̥ɛ́ patóm]
He thrice daily them watered in-order to-weave wreath for-self later
Three times every day He watered them, so that He could later make Himself a wreath.

Когда же розы расцвели, детей еврейских созвал он;
[kagdá žɛ rózy rascʋeḷí ḍeṭéj jeʋṛéjṣḳix sózval ón]
when however roses bloomed children Jewish called-together He
However, when the roses had come into bloom, he summoned the Jewish children.

Они сорвали по цветку, и сад был весь опустошён.
[aṇí sarváḷi pacʋɛtkú i sád͜ býl ʋéṣ apustašón]
they picked each-a-rose and garden was all stripped
Each of them picked a rose, leaving the garden bare.

«Как ты сплетёшь теперь венок? В твоём саду нет больше роз!»
[kák tý ṣp̣ḷeṭóš ṭep̣éṛ ʋɛnók ftvajóm sadú ṇéd͜ bóḷšɛ rós]
how You will-weave now wreath in-Your garden are-not more roses
"How will You make your wreath now? There are no more roses in Your garden."

«Вы позабыли, что шипы остались мне», сказал Христос.
[vý pazabýḷi što šypy astáḷiṣ mṇɛ́ skazál xṛistós]
you forgot that thorns remain for-me said Christ
"You have forgotten that the thorns are left for me," said Christ.

И из шипов они сплели венок колючий для него,
[i iššypóf aṇí ṣpḷeḷí ṿɛnók kaḷúc̹ij ḍḷaṇɛvó]
and from-thorns they wove wreath barbed for-Him
And out of the thorns they made for Him a prickly wreath.

И капли крови вместо роз чело украсили его.
[i káp̹ḷi króṿi vṃɛstarós c̹ɛló ukráṣiḷi jɛvó]
and drops of-blood instead-of-roses brow decorated His
And drops of blood instead of roses adorned His brow.

56. На берегу 'On the Shore' Соч. 54, № 6
(A. Pleshcheev) (1883)

1. Домик над рекою, в окнах огонёк,
[dóṃik nadṛɛkóju vóknax agaṇók]
little-house over-river in-windows light
Up from the river stands a little house. In the windows there is a light

Светлой полосою на воду он лёг.
[ṣṿέtləj palasóju návadu ón ḷók]
of-light strip onto-water it cast
Which casts a bright band onto the water.

В доме не дождутся с ловли рыбака:
[vdóṃe ṇɛdaždútca slóṿḷi rybaká]
in-house anxiously-await from-fishing fisherman
In the house all are anxiously awaiting the fisherman's return from fishing.

Обещал вернуться через два денька.
[ab̹ẹṣṣál ṿɛrnútca c̹ẹṛɛzdvá ḍeṇká]
he-promised to-return in-two days
He promised to come home in two days' time.

Но прошёл и третий, а его всё нет.
[no prašóḷ‿y ṭṛéṭij a jɛvó f̹ṣó ṇέt]
but has-passed even third and he still is-not
But the third day has already passed, and he has still not come.

Ждут напрасно дети, ждёт и старый дед.
[ždút naprásna ḍéṭi žḍót‿y stáryj ḍέt]
wait in-vain children waits also old grandfather
The children wait for him impatiently, the old grandfather, too.

Всех нетерпеливей ждёт его жена,
[f̡s̡éx n̡et̡er̡p̡el̡ív̡ej žd̡ót jɛvó žɛná]
of-all most-impatiently waits his wife
But his wife waits for him most impatiently of all.

Ночи молчаливей и, как холст, бледна...
[nóč̡i malč̡al̡ív̡ej i kak xólzd‿b̡l̡ɛdná]
than-night more-silent and like canvas pale
Silenter than midnight, as pale as a sheet...

2. Вот за ужин сели, ей не до еды:
[vód‿zaúžyn s̡él̡i jéj n̡ɛ dajɛdý]
now to-supper they-have-sat-down to-her not up-to food
Now they've sat down to dinner, but she can't eat.

«Как бы в самом деле не было беды!»
[kág‿by fsámam d̡él̡e‿n̡ébyla b̡ɛdý]
as if in-point of-fact was-none of-trouble
"If only everything can actually be all right!"

Вдоль реки несётся лодочка; на ней
[vdol̡r̡ek̡í n̡es̡ótca lódač̡ka nan̡éj]
along-river is-borne little-boat on-it
Down the river comes a small boat. From it

Песня раздаётся всё слышней, слышней.
[p̡és̡n̡a razdajótca f̡s̡ó slyšn̡éj slyšn̡éj]
song resounds ever more-audible more-audible
A song can be heard, growing louder and louder.

Звуки той знакомой песни услыхав,
[zvúk̡i tój znakóməj p̡és̡n̡i uslyxáf]
sounds of-that familiar song having-heard
Upon hearing the sounds of that familiar song,

Дети вон из дома бросились стремглав.
[d̡ét̡i vón‿yzdóma brós̡il̡is̡ s̡t̡r̡ɛmgláf]
children # out-of-house rushed headlong
The children came rushing headlong out of the house.

Весело вскочила из-за прялки мать,
[v̡és̡ɛlɑ fskɑč̡ílɑ izzɑp̡r̡álk̡i mát̡]
gaily jumped-up from-behind-spinning-wheel mother
Mother gaily leapt up from behind the spinning wheel,

И у деда силы вдруг нашлось бежать.
[i ud̡ɛ́dɑ s̡íly vdrúk n̡ɑšlóz̡‿b̡ɛžát̡]
andby-grandfather power suddenly was-found to-run
And Grandfather suddenly found the strength to run.

3. Песню заглушает звонкий крик ребят,
[p̡és̡n̡u zɑglušájɛd‿zvónkəj k̡r̡ík r̡eb̡át]
song drowns-out ringing shout of-kids
The kids' ringing shouts drown out the song.

Тщетно унимает старый дед внучат.
[t̡š̡š̡ɛ́tnɑ un̡imájɛt stáryj d̡ét vnuč̡át]
in-vain tries-to-calm old grandfather grandchildren
The old grandfather tries in vain to calm his grandchildren down.

Вот и воротился, весел и здоров!
[vót‿y vɑrɑt̡ílsɑ v̡és̡ɛl‿y zdɑróf]
here # he-has-returned happy andhealthy
Father is back at last, happy and healthy!

В россказни пустился тотчас про улов.
[vrósskɑz̡n̡i pus̡t̡ílsɑ tótč̡ɑs prɑulóf]
into-tale-telling he-launchedat-once about-catch
Immediately he launches into spinning yarns about the catch.

В морды он и в сети наловил всего.
[vmórdy ón‿y f̡s̡ét̡i nɑlɑv̡íl f̡s̡ɛvó]
in-traps he andin-nets caught all
He had caught everything in traps and nets.

С любопытством дети слушают его.
[sl̡ubɑpýtstvɑm d̡ét̡i slúšɑjut jɛvó]
with-curiosity children listen-to him
The children hang on his every word.

Смотрит дед на щуку: «Больно велика!»
[smóţŗid‿ḑét naşşúku bóļna ỵeļiká]
looks grandfather at-pike painful huge
Grandfather is looking at a pike: "It's mighty big!"

Мать сынишке в руку суёт окунька.
[máţ syņíšķɛ vrúku sujót akuņká]
mother to-son into-hand inserts perch
Mother puts a perch in the hands of her little son.

4. Девочка присела около сетей
[ḑévaçka p̧ŗişéla okalaşeţéj]
little-girl sat-down near-nets
The little girl seated herself near the nets

И взяла несмело парочку ершей.
[i ỵẓalá ņeşm̧éla páraçku jɛršéj]
and took timidly pair of-ruffs
And hesitantly picked up a couple of ruffs.

Прыгают, смеются детки, если вдруг
[prýgajut şm̧ejútca ḑétķi jéşļi vdrúk]
jump laugh children if suddenly
The children jump about, laughing, for fear that suddenly

Рыбки встрепенутся, выскользнут из рук.
[rýpķi f̧şţŗep̧ɛnútca vyskaļznút‿yzrúk]
fish will-start-to-wiggle will-slip out-of-hands
The fish will start to wiggle and will slip out of their hands

Долго раздавался смех их над рекой,
[dólga razdaválsa şm̧éx‿yx nadŗɛkój]
for-long-time resounded laughter their over-river
The laughter echoed across the river for a long time.

Ими любовался месяц золотой.
[ím̧i ļubaválsa m̧éşadz‿zalatój]
them admired moon golden
The golden moon gazed admiringly down on them.

Ласково мерцали звёзды с вышины,
[láskava m̡ɛrcá̡li z̡v̡ózdy svyšyný]
affectionately twinkled stars from-on-high
From on high the stars twinkled lovingly,

Детям обещали радостные сны.
[d̡ét̡am ab̡eš̡š̡á̡li rádasnyjɛ sný]
to-children they-promised joyous dreams
Promising the children dreams filled with joy.

57. Зимний вечер 'A Winter Evening'

(A. Pleshcheev)

Соч. 54, № 7
(1883)

Хорошо вам, детки, зимним вечерком
[xarašó vám d̡étk̡i z̡ímn̡im v̡eč̡ɛrkóm]
good for-you children on-winter evening
All is fine for you, children, on a winter evening.

В комнате уютной сели вы рядком,
[fkómnat̡ɛ ujútnəj s̡él̡i vý r̡atkóm]
in-room cozy have-sat-down you in-row
You've all seated yourselves in a row here in a cozy room.

Пламя от камина освещает вас…
[plám̡a atkam̡ína as̡v̡eš̡š̡ájɛt vás]
flame from-hearth illumines you
The fire in the hearth provides you with light.

Слушаете жадно мамы вы рассказ.
[slúšajet̡ɛ žádna mámy vý rasskás]
listen hungrily of-Mama you story
Eagerly you all listen to Mama's story.

Радость, любопытство на лице у всех,
[rádas̡t̡ l̡ubapýtstva nal̡icɛ́ uf̡s̡éx]
joy curiosity on-face by-all
Joy and curiosity shows on everyone's face.

Часто прерывает маму звонкий смех.
[č̡ásta p̡r̡ɛryvájɛt mámy zvónkəj s̡m̡éx]
often interrupts Mama ringing laughter
Mama is frequently interrupted by ringing laughter.

Вот рассказ окончен, все пустились в зал…
[vót rasskás akónç̌ɛn f̧şɛ́ puşţíļiz̧‿vzál]
now story [is] finished all have-rushed into-hall
Now the story is over, and everyone has rushed into the hall.

«Поиграй нам, мама!»-- кто-то пропищал.
[paigráj nám máma któta prap̧iş̌ş̌ál]
play for-us Mama someone squeaked
"Play something for us, Mama!" a little voice squeaks.

«Хоть уж девять било, отказать вам жаль…»
[xoţ už‿ḑév̧aḑ‿b̧íla atkazáţ vám žáļ]
although already nine has-struck to-refuse you [I am] reluctant
"Although it's already past nine, I don't have the heart to refuse…"

И послушно села мама за рояль.
[i paslúšna şɛ́la máma zarajáļ]
and obediently sat-down Mama at-piano
And Mama took her seat at the piano.

И пошло веселье! Началась возня,
[i pašló v̧eşéļjɛ naç̌aláş vazņá]
and got-underway merry-making began bustle
And the merrymaking got under way! Then began racket,

Пляска, песни, хохот, визг и беготня!
[p̧ļáska p̧éşņi xóxat v̧ísk‿y b̧ɛgatņá]
dancing songs loud-laughter squealing and running-about
Dancing, songs, loud laughter, squealing and chasing about!

Пусть гудит сердито вьюга под окном --
[púz̧ḑ‿guḑít şeŗḑíta v̧júga padaknóm]
let howl angrily blizzard beneath-window
Let the blizzard outside the windows roar angrily--

Хорошо вам, детки, в гнёздышке своём!
[xarašó vám ḑétķi vgņózdyšķɛ svajóm]
all-is-fine for-you children in-nest your
All is fine for you, children, here in your little nest.

Но не всем такое счастье Бог даёт.
[no ņe fşɛ́m takóje‿ şşáşţjɛ bóɣ‿dajót]
but not to-all such happiness God gives
But God does not give such happiness to all His creatures.

Есть на свете много бедных и сирот.
[jéşţ naşy̧éţɛ mnóga b̧ɛ́dnyx‿y şirót]
there-are in-world many poor and orphans
There are many poor people and orphans in the world.

У одних могила рано мать взяла;
[uadņíx mag̨íla rána mád̨‿y̧z̧alá]
by-some grave early mother took
Many have lost their mother to an early grave.

У других нет в зиму тёплого угла.
[udrug̨íx ņɛ́d‿vz̧ímu ţóplava uglá]
by-others is-not in-winter warm corner
Others haven't even a corner to keep warm in in winter.

Если приведётся встретить вам таких,
[jéşļi p̧ŗiy̧eḑótca fşţŗéţiţ vám tak̨íx]
if it-should-happen to-meet for-you such-people
If you should have occasion to encounter such people,

Вы, как братьев, детки, приголубьте их.
[vý kag‿bráţjɛv‿ḑɛ́tk̨i p̧ŗigalúp̧ţe‿íx]
you like brothers children be-kind-to them
You children be sure to treat them as kindly as you would your brothers.

58. Кукушка 'The Cuckoo' Соч. 54, № 8
(A. Pleshcheev, after Gellert) (1883)

«Ты прилетел из города,--
[tý p̧ŗiļeţél‿yzgórada]
you flew-here from -city
"You have flown here from the city--

Какие, скажи, там слухи носятся о нас?»
[kaķijɛ skažý tám slúx̧i nóşatca anás]
what tell there rumors circulate about-us
What sort of rumors are told there about us?"

(Скворца кукушка спрашивала раз).
[skvarcá kukúška sprášyvala rás]
starling by-cuckoo was-asked once
(The cuckoo once asked the starling.)

«Что жители толкуют городские
[štó žýţeļi talkújut garatşķijɛ]
what residents are-saying urban
"What do city dwellers say about us?

Хоть, на пример, о песнях соловья?
[xoţ nap̧ŗim̧ɛ́r ap̧éşņax salav̧já]
at-least for-instance about-songs of-nightingale
Say, for instance, about the songs of the nightingale?

Интересуюсь этим очень я».
[inţeŗɛsújuş éţim óç̌eņ já]
am-interested in-this very I
I am very interested in this."

«Весь город он приводит в восхищенье,
[v̧éz̧‿górat ón p̧ŗivóḑit vvaşx̧iş̌ş̌éņjɛ]
entire city he brings to-excitement
"He sends the whole city into raptures

Когда в саду его раздастся трель».
[kagdá fsadú jɛvó razdástca ţŗéļ]
when in-garden his will-resound trill
Whenever his trillings reverberate in a garden."

«А жаворонок?» «И жаворонка пенье
[a žávaranak i žávaranka p̧éņjɛ]
and lark and lark's song
"And the lark?" "The lark's song, too,

Пленяет очень многих». «Неужель?
[p̦l̦en̦ájɛt óč̦en̦ mnóg̦ix n̦ɛužél̦]
captivates very many really
Captivates many people." "Really?

Ну, а каков их отзыв о дрозде?»
[nú ɑ kɑkóf‿ýx ódzyf ɑdrɑz̦d̦ɛ́]
well and what their reaction to-thrush
And how do they feel about the thrush?"

«Да хвалят и его, хоть не везде».
[dɑ xvɑ́l̦ɑt‿y jɛvó xoț n̦e‿v̦ez̦d̦ɛ́]
they-praise also him though not everywhere
"He gets high praise, too, but not from everyone."

«Ещё хочу спросить я,-- может статься,
[jeș̌ș̌ó xɑč̦ú sprɑșíț jɑ móžɛt stɑ́tcɑ]
further want to-ask I could [it] happen
"I would like to ask something else. Is it possible

И обо мне ты слышал кое-что?»
[i ɑbɑmn̦ɛ́ ty slýšɑl kójɛštó]
also about-me you heard something
That you might have heard any comments about me, too?"

«Вот про тебя, сестрица, так признаться,
[vót prɑțeb̦ɑ́ șeșțr̦icɑ tɑ́k p̦r̦iznɑ́tcɑ]
now about-you sister so to-confess
"Well, about you, my sister, I must confess,

Не говорит решительно никто!»
[n̦ɛgɑvɑr̦ít r̦ɛšýțel̦nɑ n̦iktó]
does-not-speak decidedly no-one
Absolutely no one says a thing."

«А! если так,-- кукушка возопила,--
[ɑ jéșl̦i tɑ́k kukúškɑ vɑzɑp̦ílɑ]
a h if so cuckoo exclaimed
"Ah! If that is the case," exclaimed the cuckoo,

То о себе, чтоб людям отомстить,
[tó aşeb̦ɛ́ štob ļúd̦am atamşţiţ]
then about-self in-order people to-get-revenge
Then about myself, to get even with people,

Сама весь век, покуда хватит силы,
[samá v̦éş v̦ék pakúda xváţit şíly]
myself whole century while will-last strength
I for all times, as long as strength permits,

Не перестану я твердить: Куку, куку…»
[ņep̦eŗɛstánu já ţv̦eŗd̦íţ kukú kukú]
will-not-stop I to-repeat coo-coo coo-coo
Will never stop repeating coo-coo, coo-coo, coo-coo."

59. Весна 'Spring'

(A. Pleshcheev)

Соч. 54, № 9
(1883)

Уж тает снег, бегут ручьи, В окно повеяло весною…
[úš tájɛt şņɛ́g‿b̦ɛgút ruçjí vaknó pav̦éjala v̦ɛsnóju]
already thaws snow run brooks through-window wafts spring
The snow is already melting, the brooks have quickened. A spring breeze wafts in my window…

Засвищут скоро соловьи, И лес оденется листвою!
[zaşv̦íşşut skóra salav̦jí i ļɛ́s ad̦éņɛtca ļistvóju]
will-begin-to-whistle soon nightingales and woods will-dress in-foliage
Soon the nightingales will commence their songs, and the forest will dress up in greenery.

Чиста небесная лазурь. Теплей и ярче солнце стало;
[çistá ņeb̦ɛ́snaja lazúŗ ţep̦ļéj i járçɛ sóncɛ stála]
clean [is] heavenly azure warmer and brighter sun has-become
The sky is pure azure. The sun has become warmer and brighter.

Пора метелей злых и бурь Опять надолго миновала.
[pará m̦eţéļej zlýx‿y búŗ ap̦áţ nadólga m̦inavála]
time of-snowstorms evil and gales again for-long-time has-passed
The time of punishing snowstorms and gales again has passed, assuring long respite.

И сердце сильно так в груди Стучит, как будто ждёт чего-то;
[i şɛ́rtce‿şíļna tág‿vgrud̦í stuçít kag‿bútta ždót çɛvóta]
and heart strongly so in-chest pounds as if awaits something
And my heart is pounding in my chest, as if in expectation of something.

Как будто счастье впереди, И унесла зима заботы!
[kag‿bútta ʂʂáʂtjɛ fperedí i unɛslá zimá zabóty]
as if happiness [is] ahead and carried-off winter cares
As if only happiness lies in store, and all cares have left with the winter.

Все лица весело глядят. «Весна!»-- читаешь в каждом взоре.
[fsé‿líca vésɛla gladát vɛsná čitájɛš fkáždam vzórɛ]
all faces cheerfully gaze spring you-read in-every glance
Every face bears a happy expression. "It's spring!" can be read in every glance.

И тот, как празднику, ей рад, Чья жизнь -- лишь тяжкий труд и горе.
[i tót kak práznjiku jéj rát čjá žýzn liš táškəj trút‿y górɛ]
even he as-in holiday in-it [finds] joy whose life [is] only hard work and woe
Even he whose life is naught but tedious toil and woe can find joy in spring, as in a holiday.

Но резвых деток звонкий смех И беззаботных птичек пенье
[no rézvyɣ‿détag‿zvónkəj smex i bezzabótnyx ptíčɛk pénjɛ]
but of-frolicking children ringing laughter and of-carefree birds singing
But the ringing laughter of frolicking children and the singing of carefree birds

Мне говорят, кто больше всех Природы любит обновленье!
[mné gavarát któ bólše fsέx priródy lúbit abnavlénjɛ]
to-me speak who more than-anyone of-nature loves renewal
Speak most to me, who loves spring's renewal more than anyone.

60. Колыбельная песнь в бурю 'Lullabye during a Storm' Соч. 54, № 10
(A. Pleshcheev) (1883)

«Ах, уймись ты, буря! Не шумите, ели!
[áx ujmíṣ tý búra nešumíte‿jéli]
ah quiet-down you storm do-not-make-noise firs
"Ah, quiet down, storm! Hush, you firs!

Мой малютка дремлет Сладко в колыбели.
[mój malútka drémlet slátka fkalybéli]
my child dozes sweetly in-cradle
My little one is dozing sweetly in his cradle.

Ты, гроза господня, Не буди ребёнка!
[tý grazá gaspódn̦a n̦ɛbud̦í r̦eb̦ónka]
you thunderstorm of-Lord do-not-wake child
You, lightning, do not rouse my child.

Пронеситесь, тучи Чёрные, сторонкой!
[pran̦eșíțeș túç̌i ç̌órnyjɛ staronkəj]
pass-by storm-clouds black along-side
Pass us by, dark storm clouds!

Бурь ещё немало Впереди, быть может,
[búr̦ jeș̌ș̌ó n̦ɛmála fp̦er̦ed̦í býț móžɛt]
of-storms still many ahead to-be can
Perhaps many storms are on the way

И не раз забота Сон его встревожит.
[i n̦ɛráz‿zabóta són jɛvó fșțr̦ɛvóžyt]
and often care sleep his will-alarm
And cares will often disturb his slumbers.

Спи, дитя, спокойно… Вот гроза стихает;
[șp̦í d̦ițá spakójna vód‿grazá șțixájɛt]
sleep child calmly now storm grows-quiet
Sleep peacefully, my child. Now the storm abates;

Матери молитва Сон твой охраняет.
[máțer̦i mal̦ítva són tvój axran̦ájɛt]
of-mother prayer sleep your guards
Mother's prayers watch over your slumbers.

Завтра, как проснёшься И откроешь глазки,
[záftra kak prașn̦óšsa i atkrójɛž‿glásk̦i]
tomorrow when you-awake and open eyes
Tomorrow when you wake up and open your eyes

Снова встретишь солнце И любовь, и ласки!»
[snóva fșțr̦éțiš sóncɛ i l̦ubóf̦ i láșk̦i]
again [you] will-meet sun and love and caresses
You will again be greeted by the sun, and love, and caresses.

61. Цветок 'The Flower' Соч. 54, № 11
(A. Pleshcheev, after Ratisbonne) (1883)

Весело цветики в поле пестреют, Их по ночам освежает роса,
[v̦éșɛla cv̦éțik̦i fpól̦e‿p̦eșțr̦éjut íx panač̦ám așv̦ɛžájɛt rasá]
gaily flowers in-field show-colors them by-night freshen dew
The flowers in the field, refreshed by the night's dew, are gaily showing off their colors.

Днём их лучи благодатные греют, Ласково смотрят на них небеса.
[d̦n̦óm‿yx luč̦í blagadátnyjɛ g̦r̦éjut láskava smóțr̦at nan̦íx n̦eb̦ɛsá]
in-daytime them rays generous warm lovingly look on-them heavens
In the daytime abundant rays wam them, and the heavens look down on them lovingly.

С бабочкой пёстрой, с гудящей пчелою,
[zbábač̦kəj p̦óstrəj zgud̦áșșej p̦č̦ɛlóju]
with-butterfly gaudy with-buzzing bee
With the gaudy butterfly, the buzzing bee,

С ветром им любо вести разговор.
[sv̦ɛ́tram‿ým l̦úba v̦eșțí razgavór]
with-breeze to-them [is] dear to-conduct conversation
The warm breeze, they delight in conversing.

Весело цветикам в поле весною, Мил им родимого поля простор!
[v̦éșɛla cv̦éțikam fpól̦e‿v̦ɛsnóju m̦íl‿ým rad̦imava pól̦a prastór]
merry for-flowers in-field in-spring dear to-them of-native field expanse
The flowers of spring are happy in the field, whose broad expanses they adore.

Вот они видят: в окне, за решёткой, Тихо качается бледный цветок...
[vót an̦í v̦íd̦at vakn̦ɛ́ zar̦ešótkəj țíxa kač̦ájɛtca b̦l̦ɛ́dnyj cv̦ɛtók]
now they see in-window behind-bars quietly nods pale flower
Suddenly they see: on a window ledge, behind bars, a pale flower nods softly.

Солнца не зная, печальный и кроткий, Вырос он в мрачных стенах одинок.
[sónca n̦ɛznája p̦eč̦ál̦nyj i krótkəj výras ón vmráč̦nyx șțɛnáx ad̦inók]
sun not-knowing sad and gentle grew-up it within-gloomy walls alone
Sad and gentle, all alone, it grew up within gloomy walls, not knowing the sun.

Цветикам жаль его, бедного, стало, Хором они к себе брата зовут:
[cv̦éțikam žál̦ jɛvó b̦ɛ́dnava stála xóram an̦í kșeb̦ɛ́ bráta zavút]
to-flowers sorry for-him poor-one became as-choir they to-self brother call
The other flowers feel sorry for their brother and with one voice call on him to join them.

«Солнце тебя никогда не ласкало, Брось эти стены, зачахнешь ты тут!»
[sónce‿ţeb̦á n̦ikagdá n̦elaskála bróș éți șțén̦y zac̆áxn̦ɛš tý tút]
sun you never caressed abandon these walls will-wither you here
"The sun has never caressed you! Forsake these walls, you will pine away here!"

«Нет!-- отвечал он,-- хоть весело в поле, И наряжает вас ярко весна,
[n̦ét atv̦ec̆ál ón xoț v̦éșɛla fpól̦ɛ i nar̦ažájɛt vás járka v̦ɛsná]
no answered he although merry in-field and adorns you brightly spring
"No!" he replied. "Although it is fun in the field, and spring adorns you in bright colors,

Но не завидую вашей я доле И не покину сырого окна.
[nó n̦ɛzav̦íduju vášej ja dól̦ɛ i n̦ɛpak̦ínu syróva akná]
but do-not-envy your I lot and will-not-leave damp window
I do not envy you your fate and will not leave my damp window.

Пышно цветите! Своей красотою Радуйте, братья, счастливых людей.
[pýšna cv̦ețíțɛ svajéj krasatóju rádujțɛ bráțja șșașl̦ivyx l̦ud̦éj]
lushly bloom with-your beauty gladden brothers happy people
Bloom lavishly! Bring joy to happy people, my brothers!

Я буду цвесть для того, кто судьбою Солнца лишён и полей.
[já búdu cv̦éz̦d̦‿d̦l̦atavó któ sud̦bóju sónca l̦išón i pal̦éj]
I will bloom for-him who by-fate of-sun [is] deprived and of-fields
I will bloom for one who fate decrees will never see the sun or the fields.

Я буду цвесть для того, кто страдает. Узника я утешаю один.
[já búdu cv̦éz̦d̦‿d̦l̦atavó któ stradájɛt úz̦n̦ika já uțɛšáju ad̦ín]
I will bloom for-him who suffers prisoner I console alone
I will bloom for one who suffers. I alone bring consolation to this prisoner.

Пусть он, взглянув на меня, вспоминает Зелень родимых долин!»
[púșț ón vzgl̦anúf nam̦en̦á fspam̦inájɛt z̦él̦en̦ rad̦imyɣ‿dal̦in]
may he having-glanced at-me recall verdure of-native valleys
May he gaze on me and remember the rich verdure of his native vales."

62. Зима 'Winter' Соч, 54, № 12
(A. Pleshcheev) (1883)

Дед, поднявшись спозаранку, К внучкам в комнату спешит.
[d̦ét padn̦áfšyș spazaránku kvnúč̦kam fkómnatu șp̦ɛšýt]
grandfather having-arisen very-early to-grandchildren into-room hurries
Grandfather, having got up very early, rushes into his grandchildren's room.

«Доброй весточкой утешить Вас пришёл я»-- говорит.
[dobrəj v̦éstač̦kəj uțéšyț vás p̦r̦išól ja gavar̦ít]
with-good news to-placate you came I he-says
"I've brought you good news that will make you feel better," he says.

«Всё зимы вы ждали, детки, Надоела вам давно
[f̦șó z̦imý vy ždál̦i d̦étk̦i nadajéla vám davnó]
ever for-winter you waited children has-fed-up to-you long-since
"You've long been waiting for winter, kiddies, and long since have grown tired

Осень хмурая с дождями; Посмотрите-ка в окно!
[óșen̦ xmúraja zdaždd̦ám̦i pasmațr̦íțɛka vaknó]
autumn gloomy with-rains look out-window
Of gloomy rainy autumn. Well, just look out the window!

За ночь выпал снег глубокий, И мороз, как в декабре.
[zánač̦ výpal șn̦ég‿glubókəj i marós kag‿vd̦ɛkab̦r̦é]
overnight fell snow deep and frost as in-December
A deep snow has fallen during the night, and there's frost as cold as December's.

Уж впрягли в салазки Жучку Ребятишки во дворе».
[uš f̦p̦r̦agl̦í fsaláșk̦i žúč̦ku r̦eb̦ațíș̌k̦i vadvar̦é]
already harnessed to-toboggan Zhuchka kids in-courtyard
The boys in the yard have already harnessed Zhuchka to the toboggan."

И тормошит дед раскрывших глазки Сонные внучат,
[i tarmóšyd‿d̦ét raskrýfšyɣ‿gláșk̦i sónnyjɛ vnuč̦át]
and hurries grandfather having-opened eyes sleepy grandchildren
And Grandfather hurries the grandchildren, who have just opened their sleepy eyes.

Но на старого плутишки Недоверчиво глядят.
[no nastárava pluțíšk̦i n̦ɛdav̦ér̦č̦iva g̦l̦ad̦át]
but at-old-one scamps skeptically gaze
But the scamps regard the old man skeptically.

Поднял штору дед -- и точно! Снег под солнечным лучом
[pódņal štóru ḑét i tóç̌na şņékpatsólņeç̌nym luç̌óm]
raised drape grandfather andjust-so snow under-sun's ray
Grandfather raised the drape--and sure enough! Snow in the sunlight

Бриллиантами сверкает, Отливает серебром.
[b̧riļiántam̧i şv̧ɛrkájɛt atļivájɛt şeŗɛbróm]
like-diamondssparkles shot-through with-silver
Sparkled like diamonds, all shot through with silver.

«Слава Богу! Слава Богу!»-- Детки весело кричат,
[sláva bógu sláva bógu ḑétķi v̧éşɛla ķŗiç̌át]
glory to-God glory to-God kiddies gaily shout
"Hooray! Hooray!" the children shout joyfully.

А в уме их возникает Уж картин знакомых ряд:
[a vum̧é‿ix vazņikájɛt uš karţín znakómyx ŗát]
andin-mind their arises # of-pictures familiar series
And already they can picture a whole series of familiar scenes:

На салазках с гор катанье И катанье на коньках...
[nasaláskaɣ‿zgór katáņjɛ i katáņjɛ nakaņkáx]
on-toboggan downhill sledding andskating on-skates
Tobogganing down hillsides, ice skating,

И рождественская ёлка Сверху донизу в огнях!
[i raždḑéşţv̧ɛnskaja jólka şv̧érxu dóņizu vagņáx]
andChristmas tree from-top to-bottom in-lights
And a Christmas tree ablaze with lights from top to bottom.

63. Весенняя песня 'Spring Song' Соч. 54, № 13
(A. Pleshcheev) (1883)

В старый сад выхожу я. Росинки, как алмазы, на листьях блестят.
[fstáryj sát vyxažú ja raşíņķi kak almázy naļíşţjaɣ‿b̧ļeşţát]
into-old garden go-out I dew like diamonds on-leaves glistens
I go out into the old garden. The dew on the leaves glistens like diamonds,

И цветы мне головкой кивают, разливая кругом аромат.
[i cv̧ɛtý mņɛ galófkəj ķivájut raz̧ļivája krugóm aromát]
and flowers to-me head nod spilling-out around aroma
And the flowers nod their heads to me, spilling out fragrance.

Всё влечёт, веселит мои взоры: золотая пчела на цветке,
[f̧şó v̧ļeç̌ót v̧eşeļít maí vzóry zalatája p̧ç̌ɛlá nacv̧ɛtķɛ́]
everything attracts gladdens my gaze golden bee on-flower
Everything draws my eye and delights it: the golden bee on a flower,

Разноцветные бабочки крылья и синеющий лес вдалеке.
[raznacv̧ɛ́tnyjɛ bábaç̌ķi krýļja i şiņéjuş̧şij ļɛ́z‿vdaļeķɛ́]
multicolored of-butterfly wings and looming-dark-blue woods in-distance
The butterfly's multicolored wings and the forest, looming blue in the distance.

Как ярка эта зелень деревьев, купол неба как чист и глубок!
[kak jarká ɛ́ta z̧éļeņ ḑerév̧jɛf kúpal ņɛ́ba kak ç̌ist‿y glubók]
how bright [is] this verdure of-trees dome of-heaven so clean and deep
The green of the trees is so bright, the dome of heaven so clean and deep!

И брожу я, восторгом объятый, и слеза застилает зрачок.
[i bražú ja vastórgam abjátyj i şļɛzá zaşţilájɛd‿zraç̌ók]
and roam I in-ecstasy enveloped and tear clouds eye
I roam about, enveloped in ecstasy, and a tear clouds my eye.

Как любовью и радостью дышит вся природа под вешним лучом!
[kak ļubóv̧ju i rádaşţju dýšyt f̧şá p̧riróda padv̧ɛ́šņim luç̌óm]
how with-love and joy breathes all nature under-spring's ray
All of Nature pulsates with love and joy under the rays of the spring sun!

И душа благодарная чует здесь присутствие Бога во всём!
[i dušá blagadarnaja ç̌újɛt z̧ḑéş p̧ŗisútşţv̧ijɛ bóga vaf̧şóm]
and soul grateful senses here presence of-God in-everything
And my grateful soul can feel here the presence of God in all things.

64. Осень 'Autumn' Соч. 54, № 14
(A. Pleshcheev) (1883)

1. Скучная картина! Тучи без конца, Дождик так и льётся, лужи у крыльца…
[skúšnaja karțína túč̦i b̦ɛskancá dóžd̦ik tak‿y l̦jótca lúžy ukryl̦cá]
boring picture storm-clouds without-end rain just # pours puddles by-porch
What a dull scene! Storm clouds everywhere, rain pouring down, puddles by the porch…

Чахлая рябина мокнет под окном;
[č̦áxlaja r̦ab̦ína mókn̦ɛt padaknóm]
sickly mountain-ash getting-wet under-window
The wretched mountain ash grows ever wetter beneath the window,

Смотрит деревушка сереньким пятном.
[smóțr̦id‿d̦er̦ɛvúška șér̦en̦k̦im p̦atnóm]
looks village like-gray spot
The village looks like a gray smear.

Что ты рано в гости, осень к нам пришла? Ещё просит сердце света и тепла!
[štó ty rána vgóșți óșen̦ knám p̦r̦išlá jeș̌ș̌ó próșit șɛ́rtce‿șv̦ɛ́ta i țɛplá]
why you early as-guest autumn to-us have-come still asks-for heart light and warmth
Why have you come to visit us so early, autumn? My heart still begs for light and warmth!

2. Все тебе не рады! Твой унылый вид Горе да невзгоды бедному сулит.
[f̦șé‿țeb̦é‿n̦ɛrády tvój unýlyj v̦ít gór̦ɛ da n̦ɛvzgódy b̦ɛ́dnamu sul̦ít]
everyone by-you not-glad your mournful appearance woe and troubles to-poor-man promises
You bring joy to no one! Your mournful visage promises the poor man woe and troubles.

Слышит он заране крик и плач ребят:
[slýšyt ón zarán̦ɛ k̦r̦ík‿y pláč̦ r̦eb̦át]
hears he ahead-of-time crying and weeping of-kids
Already he can hear the crying of his kids,

Видит, как от стужи ночь они не спят.
[v̦íd̦it kak atstúžy nóč̦ an̦í n̦eșp̦át]
sees how from-chill at-night they do-not-sleep
He can see them, unable to sleep at night from the cold.

Нет одежды тёплой, нету в печке дров… Ты на чей же, осень, поспешила зов?
[n̦ét ad̦ɛ́ždy țópləj n̦ɛtu fp̦ɛ́č̦k̦ɛ dróf tý nač̦éj žɛ óșen̦ pașp̦ɛšýla zóf]
is-not clothing warm is-not in-stove firewood you to-whose # autumn came-rushing call
There is no warm clothing, no wood in the stove. Who summoned you so soon, autumn?

3. Вон и худ, и бледен, сгорбился больной,
[vón‿y xút‿y bḷéḍɛn zgórḅilsa baḷnój]
over-there both thin and pale bent-over sick-man
Yonder, all bent over, is the sick man, thin and pale.

Как он рад был солнцу, как был добр весной!
[kak on rád‿býl sóncu kag‿být dóbr ṿɛsnój]
how he gladdened was by-sun how was kind spring
How he enjoyed the sun, how serene he was in the spring!

А теперь наводит жёлтых листьев шум На душу больную рой зловещих дум!
[a ṭeṗéṛ navoḍit žóltyx ḷiṣṭjɛf šúm nádušu baḷnúju rój zlaṿéṣ̌ṣ̌iɣ‿dúm]
and now brings of-yellow leaves noise into-soul aching swarm of-ominous thoughts
And now the sound of the yellow leaves brings his aching soul a swarm of ominous thoughts.

Рано, рано в гости, осень, к нам пришла...
[rána rána vgóṣṭi óṣeṇ knám ṗṛišlá]
early early as-guest autumn to-us [you] have-come
Too early, too early, you've come to visit us, autumn!

Многим не дождаться света и тепла!
[mnóg̡im ṇɛdaždátca ṣṿɛ́ta i ṭɛplá]
many will-not-make-it-to light and warmth
Many will not live to see the light and warmth come back!

65. Ласточка 'The Swallow' Соч. 54, № 15
(I. Surikov, after Lenartowicz) (1883)

Идёт девочка-сиротка, тяжело вздыхает,
[iḍod‿ḍɛ́vačka ṣirótka ṭažɛló vzdyxájɛt]
goes little-girl orphan heavily sighing
A little orphan girl is walking along, sighing deeply,

А над нею, горемычной, ласточка летает.
[a nadṇéju gaṛɛmýçnəj lástačka ḷɛtájɛt]
and over-her hapless swallow flies-about
While over the poor child's head a swallow flies about.

И летает, и щебечет, над головкой вьётся,
[i l̦ɛtájɛt‿y șșeb̦éçɛt nadgalófkəj v̦jótca]
it-flies and chirps over-head flutters
It flies about over her head, chirping and fluttering,

Вьётся, крошка, и крылами в косу чуть не бьётся.
[v̦jótca króška i krylám̦i fkósu çuț n̦eb̦jótca]
it-flutters little-thing and with-wings into-hair almost beats
The tiny thing flutters about, almost beating its wings against her hair.

--Что ты вьёшься надо мною, над сироткой, пташка?
[štó ty v̦jóšsa nadamnóju natșirótkəj ptáška]
why you flutter over-me over-orphan birdie
"Why are you fluttering over me, a poor orphan, little bird?

Ах, оставь меня, и так мне жить на свете тяжко!
[áx astáf̦ m̦en̦á i ták mn̦ɛ žýț nașv̦éțe‿țáška]
ah leave me as it-is for-me to-live on-earth [is] hard
Ah, let me be! It is hard enough for me to live in this world as it is!"

--Не оставлю! Не оставлю! Буду я кружиться,
[n̦ɛastáv̦l̦u n̦ɛastáv̦l̦u búdu ja kružýtca]
I-will-not-leave [you] I-will-not-leave [you] will I to-circle
"No! I will not leave you! I will go on circling over you,

Щебетать тебе про брата, что в тюрьме томится.
[șșeb̦ɛtáț¯ țeb̦ɛ́ prabráta što fțur̦m̦ɛ́ tam̦ítca]
to-chirp to-you about-brother who in-prison languishes
Singing to you of your brother, who languishes in prison.

Он просил меня: «Слетай-ка, пташка, в край родимый,
[ón prașíl m̦en̦á șl̦ɛtájka ptáška fkráj rad̦íməj]
he begged me fly bird to-region native
He begged me: "Fly away, little bird, to my native region.

Поклонись моей сестрице, горячо любимой.
[paklan̦íș majéj șeșțr̦ícɛ gar̦açó l̦ub̦íməj]
bow to-my little-sister ardently beloved
Give my regards to my little sister, whom I love dearly

Всё ль меня она, голубка, добром вспоминает,
[fṣó ḷ mẹṇá aná galúpka dabróm fspamịnájɛt]
still # me she darling kindly remember
Does she, my darling sister, still remember me with kindness?

Всё ль она ещё о брате слёзы проливает?»
[fṣó ḷ aná jeṣṣó abrát̡ɛ ṣḷózy praḷivájɛt]
still # she still for-brother tears shed
Does she even now still shed tears for her brother?"

66. Детская песенка 'A Child's Song' Соч. 54, № 16
(K. Aksakov) (1881)

Мой Лизочек так уж мал, Что из крыльев комаришки
[mój ḷizóçɛk ták už mál što iskrýḷjɛf kamaṛíšḳi]
my Lizochek [is] so # small that from-wings of-mosquito
My Lizochek is so tiny that from mosquito wings

Сделал две себе манишки, И в крахмал!
[ẓḍɛ́lal ḍṿé‿ṣeḅɛ́ maṇíšḳi i fkraxmál]
made two for-herself shirtfronts and starched [them]
She made herself two shirtfronts--which she starched!

Мой Лизочек так уж мал, Что из грецкого ореха
[mój ḷizóçɛk ták už mál što izgṛɛ́ckava aṛɛ́xa]
my Lizochek [is] so # small that from-walnut nut
My Lizochek is so tiny that from a walnut

Сделал стул, чтоб слушать эхо, И кричал!
[ẓḍɛ́lal stúl štop slúšaṭ ɛ́xa i kṛiçál]
made chair in-order to-listen-to echo and shouted
She made herself a chair to listen to echoes in--and she shouted!

Мой Лизочек так уж мал, Что из скорлупы яичной
[mój ḷizóçɛk tak už mál što isskarlupý jaíçnəj]
my Lizochek [is] so # small that from-shell of-egg
My Lizochek is so tiny that from an eggshell

Фаэтон себе отличный Заказал!
[faɛtón ṣeḅɛ́ atḷíçnəj zakazál]
phaeton for-herself excellent ordered
She ordered made a fine phaeton for herself!

Мой Лизочек так уж мал, Что из скорлупы рачонка
[mó j ḷizóçɛk tak už mál što isskarlupý raçónka]
my Lizochek [is] so # small that from-shell of-crayfish
My Lizochek is so tiny that from a crayfish shell

Сшил четыре башмачонка И -- на бал!
[ššýl çɛtýṛɛ bašmaçónka i nabál]
sewed four shoes and off-to-ball
She made herself four shoes--and went off to a ball!

Мой Лизочек так уж мал, Что из листика сирени
[mó j ḷizóçɛk tak už mál što izḷiṣṭika ṣiṛéṇi]
my Lizochek [is] so # small that from-leaf of-lilac
My Lizochek is so tiny that from a lilac leaf

Сделал зонтик он для тени И гулял!
[ẓḍɛ́lal zónṭik on ḍḷaṭéṇi i guḷál]
made umbrella she for-shade and strolled
She made herself a parasole--and took a stroll!

Мой Лизочек так уж мал, Что, надувши одуванчик,
[mó j ḷizóçɛk tak už mál što nadúfšy aduvánçik]
my Lizochek [is] so # small that having-blown-on dandelion
My Lizochek is so tiny that she blew the down off a dandelion

Заказал себе диванчик, Тут и спал!
[zakazál ṣeḅé‿ḍivánçik tút‿y spál]
ordered herself sofa here # slept
And had a little sofa made--where she slept!

Мой Лизочек так уж мал, Что наткать себе холстины
[mó j ḷizóçɛk tak už mál što natkáṭ ṣeḅɛ́ xalṣṭíny]
my Lizochek [is] so # small that to-weave herself some-cloth
My Lizochek is so tiny that she had some cloth woven

Пауку из паутины Заказал!
[paukú ispauṭíny zakazál]
from-spider from-cobweb ordered
By a spider out of cobwebs!

67. Скажи, о чём в тени ветвей... Соч. 57, № 1
'Tell me: About what, in the branches' shade...'

(V. Sollogub) (1884)

Скажи, о чём в тени ветвей, Когда природа отдыхает,
[skažý aç̧óm fţeņí v̧eţv̧éj kagdá p̧ŗiróda addyxájɛt]
tell about-what in-shade of-branches when nature rests
Tell me: about what, in the shade of the branches, while nature is at rest,

Поёт весенний соловей, И что он песней выражает?
[pajót v̧eşéņņij salav̧éj i štó on p̧éşņej vyražájɛt]
sings spring nightingale and what he with-song expresses
Does the spring nightingale sing, and what is he telling us with his song?

Что тайно всем волнует кровь? Скажи, скажи, какое слово
[štó tájna f̧şɛ́m valnújɛt króf̧ skažý skažý kakójɛ slóva]
what secretly to-all agitates blood tell tell what word
What is it that mysteriously stirs everyone's blood? Tell me, tell me, what word

Знакомо всем и вечно ново? Любовь, любовь, любовь!
[znakóma f̧şɛ́m‿y v̧éç̧na nóva ļubóf̧ ļubóf̧ ļubóf̧]
[is] familiar to-all and [is] eternally new love love love
Is familiar to all, but is ever new? Love, love, love!

Скажи, о чём наедине, В раздумьи девушка гадает,
[skažý aç̧óm najeḑiņɛ́ vrazdúm̧ji ḑɛ́vuška gadájɛt]
tell about-what in-isolation in-meditation girl divines
Tell me, about what does the young girl dream, in pensive isolation?

Что тайным трепетом во сне Ей страх и радость обещает?
[što tájnym ţŗɛ́p̧ɛtam vaşņɛ́ jéj stráx‿y rádaşţ ab̧eş̧şájɛt]
what by-secret trembling in-dreams to-her fear and joy promises
What, with a secret thrill, promises her both fear and joy in her dreams?

Недуг тот странный назови, В котором светлая отрада,--
[ņɛdúk tót stránnyj nazav̧í fkatóram şv̧ɛ́tlaja atráda]
ailment that strange name in-which [is] bright joy
Name the strange ailment that brings radiant joy--

Чего ей ждать, чего ей надо? Любви, любви!
[ç̧ɛvó jej ždáţ ç̧ɛvó jej náda ļubv̧í ļubv̧í]
what to-her to-expect what to-her needed love love
What can she anticipate, what does she lack? Love, love!

Скажи! Когда от жизненной тоски Ты утомлённый изнываешь
[skažý kagdá adžýẓṇennəjtaṣḳi ty utaṃḷónnyj iznyvájɛš]
tell when from-life's longing you wearied pine
Tell me! When life's disappointments cause you to grow weary,

И злой печали вопреки Хоть призрак счастья призываешь,
[i zlój p̹ečáḷi vap̹ṛeḳi xoṭ p̹ṛízrak ṣ̌ṣ̌áṣṭja p̹ṛizyvájɛš]
and evil sadness despite at-least illusion of-happiness you-summon
And, despite your oppressive sadness, you seek out some illusion of happiness,

Что услаждает грудь твою? Не те ли звуки неземные,
[štó uslaždájɛd‿grúṭ⁻ tvajú ṇe‿ṭé‿ḷi zvúḳi ṇeẓɛmnýjɛ]
what charms breast your not same # sounds heavenly
What is it most charms your senses? Is it not those same celestial sounds

Когда услышал ты впервые Слова, слова любви!
[kagdá uslýšal ty f̹p̹ɛrvýjɛ slavá slavá ḷubv̹í]
when heard you for-first-time words words of-love
You heard when first you listened to words of love?

68. На нивы жёлтые... 'Onto the yellow fields...' Соч. 57, № 2
(A.K. Tolstoy) (1884)

На нивы жёлтые нисходит тишина;
[naṇívy žóltyjɛ ṇisxóḍit ṭišyná]
onto-fields yellow descends stillness
Silence falls on the yellow fields.

В остывшем воздухе от меркнущих селений,
[vastýfšɛm vózduxɛ atṃérknuṣ̌ṣ̌ix ṣeḷéṇij]
in-chilled air from-growing-dark settlements
In the chilled air, from the darkening villages,

Дрожа, несётся звон...
[dražá ṇeṣótca zvón]
trembling is-borne ringing
Trembling, the tolling of bells is heard.

Душа моя полна разлукою с тобой,
[dušá majá palná razlúkaju stabój]
soul my [is] filled by-separation from-you
My soul is filled with the pain of separation from you

И горьких сожалений,
[i góŗķix sažaļéņij]
and bitter regrets
And with bitter regrets.

И каждый мой упрёк я вспоминаю вновь,
[i káždyj mój upŗók ja fspaminaju vnóf̧]
and every my reproach I recall anew
And I again call to mind my every reproach,

И каждое твержу приветливое слово,
[i káždaje‿ţvɛŗžú pŗiy̧étļivajɛ slóva]
and every I-repeat kind word
And I again repeat every kind word

Что мог бы я сказать тебе, моя любовь,
[štó móg‿by já skazáţ¯ ţeb̧é majá ļubóf̧]
that might # I to-have-said to-you my love
That I might have said to you, my beloved,

Но что на дне души я схоронил сурово.
[no štó nadņé dušý já sxaraņíl suróva]
but that on-bottom of-soul I kept sullenly
But that I instead kept buried in my sullen soul.

69. Не спрашивай...* 'Do not ask...' Соч. 57, № 3
(A. Strugovshchikov, after Goethe) (1884)

Не спрашивай, не вызывай признанья!
[ņɛsprášyvaj ņɛvyzyváj pŗiznáņja]
do-not-ask do-not-require admission
Do not ask me, do not demand my confession!

*The speaker of this text is a woman.

Молчания лежит на мне печать;
[mɑlç̌ɑ́ņijɑ ļɛžýt nɑmņé‿p̧eç̌ɑ́ţ]
of-silence lies on-me seal
A seal of silence lies on my heart.

Всё высказать -- одно моё желанье,
[f̧şó výskɑzɑţ ɑdnó mɑjó žɛlɑ́ņjɛ]
all to-confess [is] one my desire
To tell all is my sole desire;

Но в тайне я обречена страдать!
[no ftɑ́jņe‿jɑ́ ɑb̧ŗeç̌ɛnɑ́ strɑdɑ́ţ]
but in-secret I [am] doomed to-suffer
But I am doomed to suffer in silence.

Там вечный лёд вершины покрывает,
[tɑ́m v̧éç̌nyj ļót v̧ɛršýny pɑkryvɑ́jɛt]
there eternal ice peaks covers
Yonder peaks are covered with eternal icecaps;

Здесь на поля легла ночная тень,
[z̧ḑéş nɑpɑļɑ́ ļɛglɑ́ nɑç̌nɑ́jɑ ţéņ]
here on-fields lies nocturnal shadows
Night's shade has descended on the fields;

С весною вновь источник заиграет,
[sv̧ɛsnóju vnóf̧ istóç̌ņig‿zɑigrɑ́jɛt]
with-spring again spring gushes-water
The spring again bubbles with the changing of the season;

С зарёю вновь проглянет божий день.
[zzɑŗóju vnóf̧ prɑģļɑ́ņɛd‿b̧óžyj ḑéņ]
with-dawn again will-appear God's day
A new day will burst forth with the coming of the dawn;

И всем дано в час скорби утешенье,
[i f̧şɛ́m dɑnó fç̌ɑ́s skóŗb̧i uţɛšéņjɛ]
and everyone is-given in-hour of-grief consolation
And all who mourn are granted solace in their hour of sorrow,

Указан друг, чтоб сердце облегчить:
[ukázan drúk štop ṣέrtcɛ ab̦l̦ex̧č̦iț]
designated friend in-order heart to-console
All are ordained a friend for soothing their hearts.

Мне с клятвой на устах дано одно терпенье,
[mn̦έ sk̦l̦átvǝj naustáx danó adnó țer̦p̦én̦jɛ]
to-me with-oath on-lips [is] given alone patience
I am allotted only the necessity of enduring--my lips are sealed,

И только Бог их может разрешить!
[i tól̦ka bóx íx móžɛt raz̦r̦ɛšýț]
and only God them can release
And only God can unseal them.

70. Усни 'Go to sleep' Соч. 57, № 4
(D. Merezhkovsky) (1884)

Уснуть бы мне навек в траве, как в колыбели,
[usnúḑ‿by mn̦έ navέk ftrav̦έ kak fkalyb̦él̦i]
to-fall-asleep # to-me forever in-grass as in-cradle
Would that I could fall asleep forever in the grass, as in a cradle,

Как я ребёнком спал в те солнечные дни,
[kak ja r̦eb̦ónkam spál fțέ sólņeč̦nyje‿ḑn̦í]
as I as-child slept in-those sunny days
As I slept in those sunny days when I was a child.

Когда в лучах полуденных звенели
[kagdá vluč̦áx palúḑennyɣ‿z̦v̦eņél̦i]
when in-rays noonday rang
When in the noonday sunlight there rang out

Весёлых жаворонков трели и пели мне они:
[v̦eşólyɣ‿žávarankaf țr̦él̦i i p̦él̦i mn̦έ an̦í]
of-merry larks trills and sang to-me they
The trills of merry larks singing to me:

«Усни, усни, усни...»
[uşņí uşņí uşņí]
fall-asleep fall-asleep fall-asleep
"Sleep, sleep, sleep.."

И крылья пёстрых мух с причудливой окраской
[i krýļja ņóstryx múx sņŗiçúdļivəj akráskəj]
and wings of-colorful flies with-wondrous coloring
And the wings of the bright insects with their wild colors

На венчиках цветов дрожали, как огни,
[naγéņçikax cγεtóv‿dražáļi kak agņí]
on-petals of-flowers trembled like flames
Flickered like flames on the flowers' petals,

И шум дерев казался чудной сказкой;
[i šúm ḑeŗéf kazálsa çúdnəj skáskəj]
and sound of-trees seemed like-wondrous fairy-tale
And the sounds from the trees were like fantastic fairy tales;

Мой сон лелея, с тихой лаской баюкали они:
[mój són ļeļéja sţíxəj láskəj bajúkaļi aņí]
my dreams inducing with-quiet tenderness lulled they
Inducing my dreams, with sweet tenderness they lulled me:

«Усни, усни...»
[uşņí uşņí]
fall-alseep fall-asleep
"Sleep, sleep..."

И убегая вдаль, как волны золотые,
[i uḅεgája vdáļ kak vólny zalatýjε
and running-away into-distance like waves golden
And as they fled into the distance, like waves of gold,

Давали мне приют в задумчивой тени,
[daváļi mņé‿ņŗijúd‿vzadúmçivəj ţeņí]
[they] gave me shelter in-pensive shade
I was given shelter in the dream-like shadows,

Под кущей верб, поля мои, поля родные;
[patkúşşej ɣérp paļá maí paļá radnýjɛ]
under-shelter of-pussy-willows fields my fields dear
Beneath the pussy-willows, by my beloved fields.

Склонив колосья наливные, шептали мне они:
[sklaṇíf kalóşja naļivnýjɛ šɛptáļi mṇé aṇí]
having-inclined ears ripe whispered to-me they
Lowering their ripe ears of grain over me, they whispered:

«Усни, усни...»
[uşṇí uşṇí]
fall-asleep fall-asleep
"Sleep, sleep..."

71. Смерть 'Death' Соч. 57, № 5
(D. Merezhkovsky) (1884)

Если розы тихо осыпаются,
[jéşļi rózy ţíxa asypájutca]
if roses quietly shed-petals
When roses silently let go their petals,

Если звёзды меркнут в небесах,
[jéşļi ẓɣózdy ṃérknut vṇeḅɛsáx]
if stars grow-dim in-heavens
When stars fade in the heavens,

Об утёсы волны разбиваются,
[abuţósy vólny raẓḅivájutca]
against-cliffs waves crash
And waves shatter against cliffs,

Гаснет луч зари на облаках,--
[gáşṇɛt lúḍẓ‿ẓaŗí naablakáx]
goes-out ray of-dusk on-clouds
And the last rays of dusk disappear in the clouds,

Это смерть, но без борьбы мучительной;
[éta şṃéŗţ no ḅɛzbaŗbý muçíţeļnəj]
it-is death but without-struggle torturous
It is a kind of death, but without any agonizing struggle.

Это смерть, пленяя красотой,
[ɛ́ta şm̧éŗţ p̧ļeņája krasatój]
it-is death captivating with-beauty
It is a death that enthralls with its beauty,

Обещает отдых упоительный,
[ab̧eş̌ş̌ájɛt óddyx upaíţeļnəj]
promises rest entrancing
That promises entrancing repose,

Лучший дар природы всеблагой.
[lútššyj dár p̧ŗiródy f̧şɛblagój]
better gift of-nature beneficent
Beneficent Nature's finest gift.

У неё, наставницы божественной,
[uņejó nastávņicy bažéşţv̧ɛnnəj]
by-her preceptress divine
From her, this divine preceptress,

Научитесь, люди, умирать,
[nauç̌íţeş ļúḑi um̧iráţ]
learn people to-die
Learn how to die, oh people,

Чтоб с улыбкой кроткой и торжественной,
[štop sulýpkəj krótkəj i taržéşţv̧ɛnnəj]
so-that with-smile gentle and solemn
So that you may someday, with a gentle and dignified smile,

Свой конец безропотно встречать.
[svój kaņɛ́c b̧ɛzrópatna f̧şţŗeç̌áţ]
your end unmurmuring meet
Meet your end without murmur.

72. Лишь ты один...* 'You alone...' Соч. 57, № 6
(A. Pleshcheev) (1884)

Лишь ты один в мои страданья верил,
[l̦iš tý ad̦ín vmaí stradán̦ja v̦ér̦il]
only you alone in-my sufferings believed
You alone had faith in my struggles,

Один восстал на лживый суд людской
[ad̦ín vasstál nalžývyj sút l̦utskój]
[you] alone stood-up against-false court of-men
You alone took a stand against people's false judgment of me

И поддержал мой дух изнемогавший
[i padd̦eržál moj dúx‿yzn̦emagáfšyj]
and supported my spirit exhausted
And gave succor to my exhausted spirit

В те дни, как свет во мне боролся с тьмой.
[fțé‿d̦n̦í kak șv̦ét vamn̦é barólsa sțmój]
in-those days when light within-me struggled with-darkness
In those days when the light within me struggled with the darkness.

Лишь ты один простёр мне смело руку,
[l̦iš tý ad̦ín prașțór mn̦e șm̦éla rúku]
only you alone extended to-me boldly hand
You alone boldly reached out to me

Когда к тебе, отчаянья полна,
[kagdá kțeb̦é atçájan̦ja palná]
when to-you of-despair full
When to you, filled with despair,

Пришла я с сердцем, кровью истекавшим,
[p̦r̦išlá ja sșértcem króv̦ju ișțekáfšym]
came I with-heart bleeding-to-death
I came, my heart bleeding to death,

Безжалостной толпой оскорблена.
[b̦ežžálasnəj talpój askarb̦l̦ená]
by-merciless crowd insulted
So wronged by the merciless throng.

---

*The speaker of this text is a woman.

Лишь ты один мне в жизни ни мгновенья
[l̡iš tý ad̡ín mn̡ɛ vžýz̡n̡i n̡i mgnav̡én̡ja]
only you alone to-me in-life not instant
Only you have never once in my life

Не отравлял... Один меня щадил,
[n̡ɛatrav̡l̡al ad̡ín m̡en̡á š̡š̡ad̡íl]
did-not-poison alone me have-spared
Been vindictive toward me... You alone have spared me,

Один берёг от бурь с участьем нежным...
[ad̡ín b̡er̡ók adbúr̡ suč̡ás̡t̡jɛm n̡ɛ́žnym]
[you] alone saved from-storms with-sympathy tender
You alone protected me from tumults with tender compassion...

И никогда меня ты не любил!
[i n̡ikagdá m̡en̡á ty n̡el̡ub̡íl]
and never me you not-loved
And never did you love me!

Нет! Никогда меня ты не любил...
[n̡ét n̡ikagdá m̡en̡á ty n̡el̡ub̡íl]
no never me you not-loved
No! You never loved me...

73. Вчерашняя ночь 'Last Night'

Соч. 60, № 1
(1886)

(A. Khomiakov)

Вчерашняя ночь была так светла,
[f̡č̡ɛrášn̡aja nód̡ž‿bylá tak s̡v̡ɛtlá]
last night was so light
Last night was so brilliant,

Вчерашняя ночь все звёзды зажгла
[f̡č̡ɛrášn̡aja nóč f̡s̡é‿z̡v̡ózdy zažglá]
last night all stars lit
Last night lit up all the stars

Так ясно, что, глядя на холмы и дремлющий лес,
[tak jásna što gl̦ád̦a naxólmy i d̦r̦ém̦l̦uș̌ș̌ij l̦ɛ́s]
so brightly that gazing at-hills and dozing forest
So brightly that, while gazing at the hills, at the dozing forest,

На воды, блестящие блеском небес,
[navódy b̦l̦eş̦țáș̌ș̌ije‿b̦l̦ɛ́skam ņeb̦ɛ́s]
at-waters shining with-glow of-heavens
At the waters glittering with the sky's reflection,

Я думал: о, жить в этом мире чудес
[ja dúmal o žýț vɛ́tam m̦ír̦e‿ç̌ud̦ɛ́s]
I thought oh to-live in-this world of-wonders
I thought: Oh, living in this world of wonders

Прекрасно! Прекрасны и волны и даль степей,
[p̦r̦ɛkrásna p̦r̦ɛkrásny i vólny i dál̦ ş̦țep̦éj]
[is] lovely lovely [are] both waves and distance of-steppes
Is so lovely! Lovely are the waves and great distances of the steppe;

Прекрасна в одежде зелёных ветвей
[p̦r̦ɛkrásna vad̦ɛ́žd̦e‿z̦el̦ónyx v̦ețv̦éj]
lovely in-clothes of-green branches
Lovely in its garb of green branches

Дубрава; прекрасна любовь с вечно свежим венком
[dubráva p̦r̦ɛkrásna l̦ubóf̦ sv̦ɛ́ç̌na ş̦v̦ɛ́žym v̦ɛnkóm]
[is] oak-grove lovely [is] love with-eternally fresh wreath
Is the oak-grove. Lovely is love, with its eternal freshness,

И дружбы звезда с неизменным лучом,
[i drúžby z̦v̦ɛzdá sņeizm̦ɛ́nnym luç̌óm]
and friendship's star with-unchanging ray
And friendship's bright star, with its unaltering radiance,

И песен восторг с озарённым челом,
[i p̦éş̦ɛn vastórk sazar̦ónnym ç̌ɛlóm]
and of-songs rapture with-lighted brow
And songs' rapture, with illumined brow,

И слава! Взглянул я на небо,-- там твердь ясна:
[i sláva vzgl̡anúl ja nan̡ɛ́ba tám t̡v̡ɛ́r̡t̡ jasná]
and glory glanced I at-sky there firmament [is] clear
And the glory! I glanced at the sky. There the firmament is visible:

Высоко, высоко восходит она над бездной;
[vysóka vysóka vasxód̡it aná nadb̡ɛ́znəj]
high high soars it over-abyss
High, high it soars over the abyss;

Там звёзды живые катятся в огне…
[tám z̡v̡ózdy žyvýjɛ kat̡átca vagn̡ɛ́]
there stars living roll-along in-fire
There living stars roll along in flames…

И детское чувство проснулось во мне,
[i d̡ɛ́tskaje‿č̡ústva prasnúlas̡ vamn̡ɛ́]
and childish feeling awoke in-me
And a childish emotion was aroused in me,

И думал я: лучше нам в той вышине надзвездной!
[i dúmal ja lútššɛ nám ftój vyšyn̡ɛ́ nadz̡v̡ɛ́znəj]
and thought I better for-us in-that height suprastellar
And I thought: We would be better off in that height above the stars!

74. Я тебе ничего не скажу… 'I will tell you nothing…' Соч. 60, № 2
(A. Fet) (1886)

Я тебе ничего не скажу
[ja t̡eb̡é‿n̡ič̡ɛvó n̡ɛskažú]
I to-you nothing will-not-say
I will tell you nothing.

И тебя не встревожу ничуть,
[i t̡eb̡á n̡ef̡s̡t̡r̡ɛvóžu n̡ič̡út̡]
I you will-not-alarm at-all
I will not upset you in the least.

И о том, что я молча твержу,
[i atóm što ja mólč̡a t̡v̡ɛržú]
and about-that which I silently aver
And about that which I silently repeat to myself

Не решусь ни за что намекнуть.
[n̡er̡ɛšús̡ n̡izaštó nam̡ɛknút̡]
[I] will-not-decide for-anything to-hint-at
I will never allow myself even to hint at.

Целый день спят ночные цветы,
[cɛ́lyj d̡én̡ s̡p̡át nač̡nýjɛ cv̡ɛtý]
entire day sleep nocturnal flowers
Nocturnal flowers sleep the whole day long,

Но, лишь солнце за рощу зайдёт,
[no l̡iš sóncɛ zaróš̡š̡u zajd̡ót]
but only sun behind-grove goes
But as soon as the sun ducks behind the grove,

Раскрываются тихо листы,
[raskryvájutca t̡íxa l̡istý]
unfold quietly leaves
Their leaves open silently,

И я слышу, как сердце цветёт...
[i ja slýšu kak s̡ɛ́rtcɛ cv̡et̡ót]
and I hear how heart blooms
And I can hear my heart blooming forth...

И в больную, усталую грудь
[i vbal̡núju ustáluju grút̡]
and in-pained ired breast
And into my aching, tired bosom

Веет влагой ночной... Я дрожу...
[v̡éjɛt vlágəj nač̡nój ja dražú]
wafts dampness nocturnal I tremble
Creeps the damp of the night. I tremble...

Я тебя не встревожу ничуть,
[ja t̡eb̡á n̡ef̡s̡t̡r̡ɛvóžu n̡ič̡út̡]
I you will-not-alarm at-all
I will not upset you in the least.

Я тебе ничего не скажу!
[ja ţeḅé‿ṇiçεvó ṇεskažú]
I to-you nothing will-not-say
I will tell you nothing

75. О, если б знали вы...(для тенора) Соч. 60, № 3
'Oh, if only you knew... (for tenor)'
(A. Pleshcheev) (1886)

О, если б знали вы, как много слёз незримых тот льёт,
[o jéşļi b znáļi vý kak mnóga şļós ṇezŗímyx tót ļjót]
oh if # knew you how many tears unseen he sheds
Oh, if you knew how many tears unseen are shed by him

Кто одинок, без друга и семьи,-- вы, может быть, порой
[któ aḍinóg‿ḅεzdrúga i şeṃjí vý mốžεd‿býţ parój]
who [is] alone without-friend and family you perhaps sometime
Who is alone, with neither friend nor family--perhaps you sometime

Прошли бы мимо жилища, где влачатся дни мои.
[prašļi by ṃimažyļişşa gḍε vlaçátca ḍņí maí]
pass-by would beside-domicile where drag-out days my
Would go past the domicile where my days drag by endlessly.

О, если б знали вы, что в сердце, полном тайной печали,
[o jéşļi b znáļi vý štó fşέrtcε polnam tájnəj ḅeçáļi]
oh if # knew you what in-heart full of-secret sadness
Oh, if you knew what, in a heart filled with secret sadness,

Чистый взор способен зародить,-- в моё окно порой,
[çístyj vzor spasoḅεn zaraḍíţ vmajó aknó parój]
clear gaze [is] capable to-give-rise-to into-my window sometime
An innocent gaze is capable of awakening, into my window sometime

Как бы случайно, вы, проходя, взглянули, может быть.
[kag‿by sluçájnavý vý praxaḍá vzgļanúļi mốžεd‿ḅýţ]
as if by-chance you in-passing would-glance perhaps
You perhaps would gaze, as if by chance, in passing.

О, если б знали вы, как сердцу счастья много дарит
[o jéşļi b znáļi vý kak şértcu ş̌ş̌áşţja mnóga dáŗit]
oh if # knew you how to-heart of-happiness much bestows
Oh, if you knew how much happiness is bestowed to one heart

Другого сердца близость,-- отдохнуть у моего
[drugóva şértca b̧ļizaşţ addaxnúţ umajɛvó]
of-another heart nearness to-rest by-my
By another heart's closeness--to rest by my

Вы сели бы порога, как добрая сестра, когда-нибудь.
[vy şéļi by paróga kag‿dóbraja şɛstrá kagdáņibuţ]
you sit-down would threshhold like kind sister sometime
Threshhold you might take a seat sometime, like a loving sister.

О, если б знали вы, что я люблю вас, знали, как глубоко
[o jéşļi b znáļi vý što ja ļub̧ļú váz‿znáļi kag‿glubakó]
oh if # knew you that I love you knew how deeply
Oh, if you knew that I love you, knew how deeply

Люблю, каким святым огнём вы с давних пор мне
[ļub̧ļú kaķím şy̧atým agņóm vy zdávņix pór mņɛ]
[I] love with-what holy fire you for-long time to-me
I love you, with what a holy flame you long since have been

Душу согревали, вы, может быть, ко мне вошли бы в дом!
[dúšu sagŗɛváļi vy móžed‿býţ kamņɛ́ vašļi by vdóm]
soul burned you perhaps to-me enter would into-house
Warming my soul, you perhaps would come into my house!

76. Соловей* 'The Nightingale' Соч. 60, № 4
(A. Pushkin) (1886)

Соловей мой, соловейко! Птица малая, лесная!
[salay̧éj moj salay̧éjka p̧ţica málaja ļɛsnája]
nightingale my nightingale bird little of-forest
Oh, my nightingale, my nightingale! Little bird of the forest!

---

*This text is in folk dialect.

У тебя ль, у малой птицы, незаменные три песни,
[uțeb̦ál̦ umáləj p̦țicy n̦ɛzam̦ɛ́nnyje‿țr̦í p̦éșn̦i]
by-you by-little bird irreplaceable three songs
Do you not have three unchanging songs, little bird?

У меня ли, у молодца, три великие заботы!
[um̦ená l̦i umólatca țr̦í v̦el̦ík̦ijɛ zabóty]
by-me # by-young-man three great cares
Do I, a poor young man, not have three great cares?

Как уж первая забота: рано молодца женили;
[kák uš p̦ɛ́rvaja zabóta rána mólatca žen̦íl̦i]
how # first care [too] early young-man was-married-off
My first care is this: They made me marry too young.

А вторая-то забота: ворон конь мой притомился;
[a ftarájata zabóta vóran kón̦ moj p̦r̦itam̦ílsa]
and second care black steed my has-grown-weary
My second care: My black steed is worn out.

Как уж третья-то забота: красну девицу со мною
[kák uš țr̦éțjata zabóta krásnu d̦év̦icu samnóju]
how # third care fair maiden with-me
And my third care: My maiden fair from me

Разлучили злые люди.
[razluč̦íl̦i zlýje‿l̦úd̦i]
separated wicked people
Has been taken by wicked people.

Выкопайте мне могилу во поле, поле широком,
[vykapájțɛ mn̦ɛ mag̦ilu vópol̦ɛ pól̦ɛ šyrókam]
dig me grave in-field field broad
Dig me a grave in the broad open field.

В головах мне посадите алы цветики-цветочки,
[vgalaváx mn̦ɛ pasad̦íțɛ ály cv̦éțik̦i cv̦ɛtóč̦k̦i]
at-head to-me plant scarlet flowers flowers
At my head plant flowers of scarlet.

А в ногах мне проведите чисту воду ключевую.
[a vnagáx mn̦ɛ pravḙḍițḙ‿č̦istu vódu k̦l̦uč̦ɛvúju]
and at-feet to-me provide clean water from-spring
And at my feet provide clean spring water.

Пройдут мимо красны девки,
[prajdút m̦íma krásny ḍɛ́fk̦i]
[whenever] will-pass by fair maids
Whenever fair maids pass by,

Так сплетут себе веночки.
[tak ș̦p̦l̦ɛtút ș̦eb̦é‿v̦ɛnóč̦k̦i]
so they-will-weave themselves little-wreaths
They will weave themselves little crowns of flowers.

Пройдут мимо стары люди, так воды себе зачерпнут.
[prajdút m̦íma stáry l̦úḍi tak vadý ș̦eb̦ɛ́ zač̦ɛ́rpnut]
[whenever] will-pass by old people so water themselves will-dip
Whenever old people pass by, they will dip themselves up some water.

77. Простые слова 'Simple Words'

(P. Tchaikovsky)

Соч. 60, № 5
(1886)

Ты--звезда на полночном небе,
[tý z̦v̦ɛzdá napalnóč̦nam n̦éb̦ɛ]
you [are] star in-midnight sky
You are a star in the midnight sky,

Ты--весенний цветок полей;
[tý v̦eș̦én̦n̦ij cv̦ɛtók pal̦éj]
you [are] spring flower of-fields
You are a sweet field-flower in spring.

Ты--рубин иль алмаз блестящий,
[tý rub̦ín il̦ almáz‿b̦l̦eș̦ţáș̦ș̦ij]
you [are] ruby or diamond gleaming
You are a shining ruby, a diamond.

Ты--луч солнца, во тьме светящий,
[tý lúč̦ sónca vaţm̦é‿ș̦v̦eţáș̦ș̦ij]
you [are] ray of-sun in-darkness shining
You are a ray of sunlight in the darkness,

Чаровница и царица красоты.
[ç̌araɣ̧ņíca i caŕ̨ica krasatý]
enchantress and queen of-beauty
An enchantress and queen of beauty.

Так по струнам бряцая лирным,
[ták pastrúnam b̧r̨acája ļ́irnym]
thus along-strings thrumming of-lyre
Thus, thrumming the strings of their lyres,

Тьмы певцов о тебе поют.
[ţmý p̧ɛfcóf aţeb̧ɛ́ pajút]
thousands of-singers of-you sing
Hosts of poets sing your praises.

Славы нектар тобой изведан,
[slávy ņɛ́ktar tabój iẓɣ̧ɛ́dan]
of-glory nectar by-you has-been-experienced
You have tasted the nectar of fame.

Мне ж дар песен от Бога не дан,
[mņɛ́ ž dár p̧éşɛn adbóga ņɛ́ dan]
to-me but gift of-songs from-God has-not-been-given
But I have not been blessed by God with the gift of song.

Я простые скажу слова:
[já prastýjɛ skažú slavá]
I simple will-say words
I will utter only these simple words:

«Ты--мой друг, ты моя опора,
[tý mój drúk tý majá apóra]
you [are] my friend you [are] my support
"You are a friend to me, you are my strength;

Ты мне жизнь, ты мне все и всё…
[tý mņɛ́ žýẓņ tý mņɛ́ f̧şé‿i f̧şó]
you to-me [are] life you to-me [are] everyone and everything
You are my life, you are everything and everybody to me.

Ты мне воздух и хлеб насущный,
[tý mn̦ɛ́ vózdux‿y x̦l̦ɛ́p nasúș̌ș̌nyj]
you [are] to-me air and bread daily
You are the air I breathe, my daily bread;

Ты двойник мой единосущий,
[tý dvajn̦ík mój jed̦inasúș̌ș̌ij]
you [are] double my of-one-essence
You are my other self, sharing my essence;

Ты--отрада и услада дней моих!...»
[tý atráda i usláda d̦n̦éj maíx]
you [are] joy and delight of-days my
You are the joy and delight of all my days."

Пусть по струнам бряцая лирным,
[púș̦ț̦ pastrúnam b̦r̦acája l̦írnym]
let on-strings thrumming of-lyres
Let it be so that, thrumming the strings of their lyres,

Тьмы певцов о тебе поют...
[ț̦mý p̦ɛfcóf aț̦eb̦ɛ́ pajút]
thousands of-singers of-you sing
Hosts of poets sing your praises.

Славы нектар тобой изведан;
[slávy n̦ɛ́ktar tabój iz̦v̦ɛ́dan]
of-glory nectar by-you has-been-experienced
You have tasted the nectar of fame.

Мне ж дар песен от Бога не дан,
[mn̦ɛ́ ž dár p̦éș̦ɛn adbóga n̦ɛ́ dan]
to-me but gift of-songs from-God has-not-been-given
But I have not been blessed by God with the gift of song.

Как сумел, так и сказал!...
[kák sum̦ɛ́l ták‿y skazál]
as I-could so just spoke
I spoke as I was able.

78. Ночи безумные 'Nights of Madness'
(A. Apukhtin)

Соч. 60, № 6
(1886)

Ночи безумные, ночи бессонные,
[nóçi ḅɛzúmnyjɛ nóçi ḅɛssónnyjɛ]
nights insane nights sleepless
Nights of madness, nights of sleeplessness,

Речи несвязные, взоры усталые…
[ŗéçi ņeşṿáznyjɛ vzóry ustályjɛ]
speeches disjointed gazes weary
Unconnected utterances, weary gazes…

Ночи, последним огнём озарённые,
[nóçi paşļéḑņim agņóm azaŗónnyjɛ]
nights by-last flame lit
Nights illumined by the last flickering flame,

Осени мёртвой цветы запоздалые!
[óşeņi ṃórtvəj cṿɛtý zapazdályjɛ]
of-autumn dead flowers belated
The belated blooms of dead autumn!

Пусть даже время рукой беспощадною
[púẓḑ‿dáže‿ṿŗéṃa rukój ḅɛspaşşádnaju]
let even time with-hand merciless
Never mind that even time itself, with an unmerciful hand,

Мне указало, что было в вас ложного,
[mņɛ́ ukazála štó býla vvás lóžnava]
to-me indicated what was in-you false
Has shown me the falseness that was in you;

Всё же лечу я к вам памятью жадною,
[fşó že‿ļeçú ja kvám páṃaţju žádnaju]
still # fly I to-you in-memory hungry
Still I fly to you in my mind, hungrily,

В прошлом ответа ищу невозможного…
[fpróšlam atṿɛ́ta işşú ņevazmóžnava]
in-past answer [I]-seek impossible
Seeking impossible solutions in the past…

Вкрадчивым шёпотом вы заглушаете
[fkrátçivym šópatam vý zaglušájetɛ]
with-insinuating whisper you muffle
With suggestive whispers you drown out

Звуки дневные, несносные, шумные...
[zvúķi d̡n̡ɛvnýjɛ n̡ɛsnósnyjɛ šúmnyjɛ]
sounds of-day unbearable noisy
The insufferable, noisy sounds of daily life.

В тихую ночь вы мой сон отгоняете,
[ft̡íxuju nóç vy moj són adgan̡ájet̡ɛ]
in-quiet night you my sleep drive-off
In the silence of the night you give me no rest,

Ночи бессонные, ночи безумные!
[nóçi b̡ɛssónnyjɛ nóçi b̡ɛzúmnyjɛ]
nights sleepless nights insane
Nights of sleeplessness, nights of madness.

79. Песнь цыганки* 'Song of the Gypsy-girl' Соч. 60, № 7
(Ya. Polonsky) (1886)

Мой костёр в тумане светит, Искры гаснут на лету...
[mój kaşt̡ór ftumán̡e‿şv̡ét̡it ískry gásnut nal̡ɛtú]
my campfire in-fog burns sparks go-out in-flight
My campfire glows in the mists, sparks fly up and go out...

Ночью нас никто не встретит; Мы простимся на мосту.
[nóçju nás n̡iktó n̡efşt̡r̡ét̡it mý praşt̡ímsa namastú]
at-night us no-one will-not-meet we will-say-goodbye on-bridge
We will encounter no one in the night, as we say goodbye on the bridge.

Ночь пройдёт, и спозаранок В степь, далёко, милый мой,
[nóç prajd̡ót‿y spazarának fşt̡éb̡‿dal̡óka m̡ílyj mój]
night will-pass and very-early into-steppe far-away dearest mine
When the night has past, very early, off onto the steppe, far away, my dearest,

---

*The speaker of this text is a woman.

Я уйду с толпой цыганок За кибиткой кочевой.
[ja ujdú stalpój cygának zaķib̧itkəj kaç̌εvój]
I will-leave with-crowd of-Gypsy-women behind-cart nomadic
I will leave with a crowd of Gypsy women, walking behind a nomad's cart.

На прощанье шаль с каймою Ты на мне узлом стяни:
[napraş̌ş̌áņjε šáļ skajmóju ty namņέ uzlóm şţaņí]
in-parting shawl with-fringe you on-me in-knot tie
As a parting gift, knot around me a fringed shawl.

Как концы её, с тобою Мы сходились в эти дни.
[kak kancý jejó stabóju my sxaḑíļiş véţi ḑņí]
like corners its with-you we were-joined in-these days
Like its corners, we have been joined together in these days.

Кто-то мне судьбу предскажет? Кто-то завтра, сокол мой,
[któta mņέ suḑbú p̧ŗεtskážεt któta záftra sókal mój]
who to-me destiny will-foretell who tomorrow falcon mine
Who will predict my future? Who will tomorrow, my falcon

На груди моей развяжет Узел, стянутый тобой?
[nagruḑí majéj razv̧ážεt úz̧εl şţánutyj tabój]
on-breast my will-untie knot tied by-you
Loose the knot on my breast that you tied?

Вспоминай, коли другая, Друга милого любя,
[fspam̧ináj koļí drugája drúga m̧ílava ļub̧á]
remember if another friend dear loving
Remember me when another woman, showing love to you, my darling,

Будет песни петь, играя На коленях у тебя!
[búḑεt p̧éşņi p̧éţ igrája nakaļéņjax uţeb̧á]
will songs sing playing on-knees by-you
Playfully sings songs to you while sitting on your lap.

80. Прости! 'Farewell!' Соч. 60, № 8
(N. Nekrasov) (1886)

Прости! Не помни дней паденья, Тоски, унынья, озлобленья,
[praşţí ņεpómņi ḑņéj paḑéņja taşķí unýņja azlab̧ļéņja]
farewell do-not-remember days of-dejection of-anguish of-depression of-malice
Farewell! Remember not the days of dejection, anguish, depression, and malice.

Не помни бурь, не помни слёз, Не помни ревности угроз!
[ņɛpómņi búŗ ņɛpómņi şļós ņɛpómņi ŗévnaşţi ugrós]
do-not-remember storms do-not-remember tears do-not-remember of-jealousy threat
Remember not the outbursts, remember not the tears, remember not my jealous threats.

Но дни, когда любви светило Над нами ласково всходило
[no ḑņí kagdá ļubvi şvɛţíla nadnáṃi láskava fsxaḑíla]
but days when love's sun over-us lovingly ascended
Remember rather the days when love's sun shone brightly and reigned over us tenderly,

И бодро мы свершали путь,-- Благослови и не забудь!
[i bódra mý şvɛršáļi púţ blagaslaví i ņɛzabúţ]
and robustly we conducted journey bless and do-not-forget
And we strode toward the future boldly. Bless those days and forget them not!

81. Ночь 'Night'

(Ya. Polonsky)

Соч. 60, № 9
(1886)

Отчего я люблю тебя, светлая ночь?
[atçɛvó ja ļubļú ţeḅá şvétlaja nóç]
why I love you bright night
Why do I love you, luminous night?

Так люблю, что, страдая, любуюсь тобой!
[tak ļubļú što stradája ļubújuş tabój]
so [I]-love that suffering [I]-admire you
Love you so much, that my admiration causes me suffering?

И за что я люблю тебя, тихая ночь?
[i zaštó ja ļubļú ţeḅá ţíxaja nóç]
and for-what I love you quiet night
And what do I love you for, silent night?

Ты не мне, ты другим посылаешь покой!
[ty ņɛ mņé ty druģím pasylájɛš pakój]
you not to-me you to-others send peace
You send others peace, but none to me!

Что мне звёзды, луна, небосклон, облака,
[štó mn̹e͜z̹v̹ózdy luná n̹ebasklón ablaká]
what to-me stars moon heaven's-vault clouds
What are the stars, the moon, the vault of the heavens, the clouds to me?

Этот свет, что, скользя на холодный гранит,
[ɛ́tat s̹v̹ɛ́t što skal̹z̹á naxalódnyj gran̹ít]
this light which tripping onto-cold granite
This light which, tripping onto cold granite,

Превращает в алмазы росинки цветка
[p̹r̹ɛvraš̹š̹ájɛt valmázy ras̹ínk̹i cv̹ɛtká]
transforms into-diamonds dew of-flower
Tranforms the dewdrops on flowers into diamonds

И, как путь золотой, через море бежит!
[i kak púd̹͜zalatój č̹er̹ɛzmór̹e͜b̹ɛžýt]
and like path golden through-sea runs
And races across the sea in a path of gold.

Ночь, за что мне любить твой серебряный свет?
[nód̹ž̹͜zaštó mn̹e͜l̹ub̹ít̹ tvój s̹er̹éb̹r̹anyj s̹v̹ɛ́t]
night, why to-me to-love your silvery light
Night, why should I love your silvery light?

Усладит ли он горечь скрываемых слёз?
[uslad̹ít l̹i on gór̹eč̹ skryvájɛmyx s̹l̹ós]
will-sweeten # it bitter-taste of-concealed tears
Will it sweeten the bitter taste of my concealed tears?

Даст ли жадному сердцу желанный ответ,
[dást l̹i žádnamu s̹értcu žɛlánnyj atv̹ɛ́t]
will-give # to-hungry heart desired answer
Will it give my hungering heart the answer it longs for?

Разрешит ли сомнений тяжёлый вопрос?
[raz̹r̹ɛšýt l̹i samn̹én̹ij t̹ažólyj vaprós]
will-decide # of-doubts heavy question
Will it solve the oppressive enigma of my doubts?

Сам не знаю, за что я люблю тебя, ночь,
[sám ņɛznáju zaštó ja ļuḅļú ţeḅá nóç̌]
myself do-not-know why I love you night
I myself do not know why I love you, night;

Так люблю, что, страдая, любуюсь тобой!...
[ták ļuḅļú što stradája ļubújuş tabój]
so [I]-love that suffering [I]-admire you
Love you so much, that my admiration causes me suffering!

Сам не знаю, за что я люблю тебя, ночь...
[sám ņɛznáju zaštó ja ļuḅļú ţeḅá nóç̌]
myself do-not-know why I love you night
I myself do not know why I love you, night;

Оттого, может быть, что далёк мой покой.
[attavó móžɛd‿ḅýţ što daļók mój pakój]
because perhaps that [is] far my peace
Perhaps it is because my peace is so very far away

82. За окном в тени мелькает 'Inside the dark window flashes...' Соч. 60, № 10
(Ya. Polonsky) (1886)

За окном в тени мелькает русая головка.
[zaaknóm fţeņí ṃeļkájɛt rúsaja galófka]
inside-window in-shade glistens brown head
Inside the window a brown head of hair glistens in the darkness.

Ты не спишь, моё мученье! Ты не спишь, плутовка!
[ty ņeşp̧íš majó muç̌éņjɛ ty ņeşp̧íš plutófka]
you do-not-sleep my misery you do-not-sleep little-rogue
You're not asleep, my tormenter! You're not asleep, little rogue!

Выходи ж ко мне навстречу! С жаждой поцелуя,
[vyxaḍí š kamņɛ́ nafşţŗéç̌u žžáždəj pacɛlúja]
come-out # to-me in-meeting with-thirst for-kiss
Come out to meet me! Hungering for your kiss,

К сердцу сердце молодое пламенно прижму я.
[kşértcu şértcɛ maladójɛ plámɛnna pŗižmú ja]
to-heart heart young ardently will-press I
I will press your young heart ardently to my own.

Ты не бойся, если звёзды слишком ярко светят:
[ty ņɛbójsa jéşļi zvózdy şļiškam járka şvéţat]
you do-not-fear if stars too brightly shine
Don't be afraid if the stars seem to shine too brightly:

Я плащом тебя одену, так что не заметят.
[ja plaşşóm ţeþá adénu ták što ņezamétat]
I with-cloak you will-dress so that [they]-will-not-notice
I will put my cloak over you, so that no one will notice.

Если сторож нас окликнет,-- назовись солдатом;
[jéşļi stóraš nás akļíkņɛt nazavíş saldátam]
if sentry us calls-out-to call-yourself soldier
If a sentry should call out to us, claim to be a soldier.

Если спросят, с кем была ты,-- отвечай, что с братом.
[jéşļi spróşat şkém bylá ty atvɛčáj što zbrátam]
if [they]-will-ask with-whom were you answer that with-brother
If you are asked who you were with, say it was your brother.

Под надзором богомолки ведь тюрьма наскучит,
[padnadzóram bagamólķi veţ¯ ţuŗmá naskúčit]
under-surveillance of-woman-penitent you-know prison will-bore
Being in a prison under a nun's watchful eye can become boring, after all;

А неволя поневоле хитрости научит.
[a ņɛvóļa paņɛvóļɛ xitraşţi naúčit]
and captivity willy-nilly craftiness teaches
And captivity teaches cunning, willy-nilly.

83. Подвиг (Монолог для баритона) Соч. 60, № 11
'Heroism (Monologue for Baritone)'
(A. Khomiakov) (1886)

Подвиг есть и в сраженьи, Подвиг есть и в борьбе,--
[pódv̦ik jéșț i fsražén̦ji pódv̦ik jéșț i vbar̦b̦ɛ́]
heroism there-is both in-battle heroism there-is and in-struggle
There is heroism in battle, and there is heroism in struggle.

Высший подвиг в терпеньи, Любви и мольбе.
[výššyj pódv̦ik fțer̦p̦én̦ji l̦ubv̦í i mal̦b̦ɛ́]
highest heroism [is] in-patience love and supplication
But the ultimate heroism is to be found in patience, love, and supplication.

Если сердце заныло Перед злобой людской,
[jéșl̦i șɛ́rtcɛ zanýla p̦er̦ɛdzlóbəj l̦utskój]
if heart aches before-malice of-people
If your heart aches from the malice of men,

Иль насилье схватило Тебя цепью стальной,
[il̦ nașíl̦jɛ sxvațíla țeb̦á cép̦ju stal̦nój]
or violence has-bound you with-chain of-steel
Or violence has bound you with its steel chains,

Если скорби земные Жалом в душу впились,
[jéșl̦i skór̦b̦i z̦ɛmnýjɛ žálam vdúšu fp̦il̦íș]
if sorrows earthly like-sting into-soul have-pierced
If earthly sorrows have pierced your soul like a dart,

С верой бодрой и смелой Ты за подвиг берись:
[sv̦ɛ́rəj bódrəj i șm̦ɛ́ləj ty zapódv̦ig‿b̦er̦íș]
with-faith robust and bold you heroism undertake
With faith sure and true, accomplish your own heroism.

Есть у подвига крылья, И взлетишь ты на них
[jéșț upódv̦iga krýl̦ja i v̦z̦l̦ețíš ty nan̦íx]
there-are by-heroism wings and will-fly-upward you on-them
Heroism has wings which will bear you upward,

Без труда, без усилья Выше мраков земных;
[b̦ɛstrudá b̦ɛzușíl̦ja výšɛ mrákav‿z̦ɛmnýx]
without-strain without-exertion higher than-gloom of-earth
Easily, effortlessly, higher than earth's dreariness,

Выше крыши темницы, Выше злобы слепой,
[výšɛ krýšy ţem̦ņícy výšɛ zlóby şļɛpój]
higher than-roof of-dungeon higher than-malice blind
Higher than the dungeon's roof, higher than blind malice,

Выше воплей и криков Гордой черни людской!
[výšɛ vópļej i ķŗíkaf górdəj ҫ̦éŗņi ļutskój]
higher than-screams and cries of-proud mob of-people
Higher than the howls and shouts of the common herd!

84. Нам звёзды кроткие сияли... 'The stars shone gently...' Соч. 60, № 12
(A. Pleshcheev) (1886)

Нам звёзды кроткие сияли, Чуть веял тихий ветерок,
[nám z̦v̦ózdy krótķije‿şijáļi ҫ̦úţ v̦éjal ţíxəj v̦eţɛrók]
for-us stars gentle shone barely wafted quiet breeze
The stars shone gently down on us. A quiet breeze was barely discernible.

Кругом цветы благоухали, И волны ласково журчали У наших ног.
[krugóm cv̦ɛtý blagauxáļi i vólny láskava žurҫ̦áļi unášyx nók]
all-about flowers gave-off-fragrance and waves lovingly murmured at-our feet
The fragrance of flowers filled the air, and waves lapped lovingly at our feet.

Мы были юны, мы любили, И с верой вдаль смотрели мы;
[my býļi júny my ļub̦íļi i sv̦érəj vdáļ smaţŗéļi mý]
we were young we loved and with-faith into-distance looked we
We were young and in love; and with confidence we faced the future.

В нас грёзы радужные жили, И нам не страшны вьюги были Седой зимы.
[vnáz‿g̦ŗózy rádužnyjɛ žýļi i nám ņɛ strášny v̦júg̦i býļi şɛdój z̦imý]
in-us dreams rainbow-like lived and to-us not-terrible blizzards were of-gray winter
Rainbow-hued dreams were within us, and we were not afraid of the blizzards of hoary winter.

Где ж эти ночи с их сияньем, С благоухающей красой,
[gd̦ɛ́ ž éţi nóҫ̦i sýx şijáņjɛm zblagauxájuşşej krasój]
where # [are] those nights with-their glow with-fragrant beauty
What has become of those nights with their aura, with their fragrant beauty,

И волн таинственным журчаньем, Надежд, восторженных мечтаний
[i vóln taínşţv̦ɛnnym žurҫ̦áņjɛm nad̦ɛ́št vastóržɛnnyx m̦ɛҫ̦táņij]
and of-waves with-mysterious murmuring of-hopes of-rapturous dreams
With the waves' mysterious murmuring? Of hopes and rapturous dreams

Где светлый рой?
[gd̦é‿șv̦ɛ́tlyj rój]
where [is] bright swarm
Where are the radiant rushes?

Померкли звёзды, и уныло Поникли блёклые цветы…
[pam̦ɛ́rk̦l̦i z̦v̦ózdy i unýla pan̦ík̦l̦i b̦l̦óklyjɛ cv̦ɛtý]
have-grown-dim stars and gloomily have-drooped faded flowers
The stars have grown dim, the faded flowers have sadly drooped down…

Когда ж, о сердце, всё, что было Что нам весна с тобой дарила, Забудешь ты?
[kagdá ž o șɛ́rtcɛ f̦șó što býla štó nám v̦ɛsná stabój dar̦íla zabúd̦ɛš tý]
when # oh heart all that was that to-us spring with-you bestowed will-forget you
When will my heart be able to forget all that we had, all that spring bestowed upon us?

85. Я сначала тебя не любила…* 'At first I did not love you…' Соч. 63, № 1
(K.R.) (1887?)

Я сначала тебя не любила, Ты тревожил меня и пугал:
[ja snaçála țeb̦á n̦el̦ub̦ila ty țr̦ɛvóžyl m̦en̦á i pugál]
I at-first you did-not-love you alarmed me and frightened
At first I did not love you. You alarmed and frightened me.

Меня новая участь страшила, И неведомый жребий смущал.
[m̦en̦á nóvaja úçașț strašýla i n̦ev̦ɛ́damyj žr̦éb̦ij smuşşál]
me new fate terrified and unknown destiny confused
My new lot in life terrified me, my unknown destiny confused me.

Твоего я боялась признанья… Но настал неминуемый час,
[tvajɛvó ja bajálaș p̦r̦iznán̦ja no nastál n̦em̦inújɛmyj çás]
your I feared declaration but arrived inevitable hour
I feared your declaration of love… But the inevitable hour arrived,

И, не помня себя, без сознанья, Я навеки тебе отдалась.
[i n̦ɛpómn̦a șeb̦á b̦ɛssaznán̦ja ja nav̦ék̦i țeb̦ɛ́ addaláș]
and not-remembering myself unconscious I forever to-you gave-myself
And I, bereft of memory and consciousness, gave myself to you forever.

*The speaker of this text is a woman.

И рассеялись вновь опасенья, Прежней робости нет и следа:
[i rasşéjaļiş vnóf̧ apaşéņja p̧r̦éžņej róbaşţi ņét͜y şļɛdá]
and vanished anew misgivings of-former timidity there-was-not even trace
And all my misgivings suddenly vanished, leaving no trace of my former shyness.

Под лучами зари во мгновенье Так туманная тает гряда.
[padluçáņi zar̦i vamgnaɣéņjɛ ták tumánnaja tájɛd͜g̦r̦adá]
under-rays of-dawn in-instant thus of-fog dissipates bank
Just as a bank of fog dissipates in an instant at the dawn's first rays,

Словно солнце, любовь просияла, И немеркнущий день заблистал.
[slóvna sóncɛ ļubóf̧ praşijála i ņeņérknuşşij d̦éņ zab̦listál]
like sun love shone-forth and unfading day blazed-forth
Like the morning sun, love burst forth, and the brilliant new day shone radiantly.

Жизнью новою сердце взыграло, И священный огонь запылал.
[žýz̧ņju nóvaju şértcɛ vzygrála i şɣaşşénnyj agóņ zapylál]
with-life new heart leapt and sacred flame flared-up
My heart surged with a new life, and a sacred flame flared up.

86. Растворил я окно... 'I opened the window wide...' Соч. 63, № 2
(K.R.) (1887)

Растворил я окно -- стало душно невмочь,--
[rastvar̦íl ja aknó stála dúšna ņɛvmóç]
opened I window had-become stuffy unbearably
I opened wide the window. It had become unbearably stuffy.

Опустился пред ним на колени,
[apuşţílsa p̧r̦ɛdņím nakaļéņi]
lowered-myself before-it onto-knees
I knelt down before it.

И в лицо мне напухла весенняя ночь
[i vļicó mņɛ napúxla ɣeşéņņaja nóç]
and into-face to-me wafted spring night
And the spring night came wafting into my face

Благовонным дыханьем сирени.
[blɑgɑvónnym dyxɑ́n̡jɛm s̡ir̡én̡i]
with-fragrant breath of-lilacs
With the fragrant aroma of lilacs.

А вдали где-то чудно запел соловей;
[ɑ vdɑl̡í gd̡ɛ́tɑ ç̌údnɑ zɑp̡ɛ́l sɑlɑv̡éj]
and far-off somewhere wondrously sang nightingale
Somewhere far away a nightingale burst into wondrous song;

Я внимал ему с грустью глубокой…
[jɑ v̡n̡imɑ́l jɛmú zgrús̡t̡ju glubókəj]
I harked to-him with-sadness deep
I harked to his song, deeply saddened.

И с тоскою о родине вспомнил своей;
[i stɑskóju ɑród̡in̡ɛ spómn̡il svɑjéj]
and with-longing about-homeland [I] recalled my
And with longing I recalled my homeland.

Об отчизне я вспомнил далёкой,
[ɑbɑtç̌íz̡n̡e‿jɑ fspómn̡il dɑl̡ókəj]
about-homeland I recalled distant
I recalled the distant land of my birth,

Где родной соловей песнь родную поёт
[gd̡ɛ́ rɑdnój sɑlɑv̡éj p̡és̡n̡ rɑdnúju pɑjót]
where native nightingale song native sings
Where our native nightingale sings its own song

И, не зная земных огорчений,
[i n̡ɛznɑ́jɑ z̡ɛmnýx ɑgɑrç̌én̡ij]
and not-knowing earthly grievances
And, unaware of the pain of earthly existence,

Заливается целую ночь напролёт
[zɑl̡ivɑ́jɛtsɑ cɛ́luju nóç̌ nɑprɑl̡ót]
pours-forth entire night long
Pours forth melodies all night long

Над душистою веткой сирени...
[naddušýstaju v̧étkəj şir̦én̦i]
over-fragrant branch of-lilacs
Above its branch of fragrant lilacs...

87. Я вам не нравлюсь... 'I do not please you...' Соч. 63, № 3
(K.R.) (1887)

Я вам не нравлюсь... Вы любили Лишь дружбу -- не любовь мою.
[já vám ņɛnráv̧ļuş vý ļub̦íļi ļiž‿drúžbu ņe‿ļubóf̦ majú]
I to-you am-not-pleasing you loved only friendship not love my
I do not please you... You liked only my friendship, not my love.

Мои надежды вы сгубили,-- И всё-таки я вас люблю!
[maí nad̦ɛ́ždy vy zgub̦íļi i f̦şótak̦i já vás ļub̦ļú]
my hopes you destroyed and nevertheless I you love
You have destroyed all my hopes, but I love you nonetheless.

Когда же после как-нибудь Поймёте вы мои мученья,
[kagdá žɛ póşļɛ kakņibúţ pajm̦óţɛ vý maí muç̌éņja]
when # afterward sometime come-to-understand you my torments
But sometime in the future, when you come to understand my torments,

И незаметно в вашу грудь Проникнет капля сожаленья,--
[i ņɛzam̦étna vvášu grúţ praņíkņɛt kápļa sažaļéņja]
and unwittingly into-your breast will-penetrate droplet of-regret
And unwittingly a spark of regret slips into your heart--

То будет поздно... Расцветают Лишь раз весенние цветы;
[to búd̦ɛt pózna rascv̧ɛtájut ļiš rás v̧eşéņņijɛ cv̧ɛtý]
then will-be [too] late bloom only once spring flowers
But it will be too late. The flowers of spring bloom but once;

Уж сердца вновь не приласкают Перестрадавшие мечты.
[uš şértca vnóf̦ ņep̦rilaskájut p̦er̦ɛstradáfšyjɛ m̦eç̌tý]
heart anew will-not-move having-suffered-much dreams
A heart cannot be moved anew by dreams already dashed.

88. Первое свидание 'First Meeting' Соч. 63, № 4
(K.R.) (1887)

Вот миновала разлука унылая, Пробил свидания час,
[vót m̡inaválа razlúka unýlaja próbil s̡v̡idán̡ija c̡ás]
now has-passed separation cheerless has-sounded of-reunion hour
Our cheerless separation is now over. The hour of reunion has sounded.

Светлое, полное счастие, милая, Вновь наступило для нас.
[s̡v̡étlajɛ pólnaje‿s̡s̡ás̡t̡ije‿m̡ilaja vnóf̡ nastup̡ila d̡l̡anás]
bright full happiness dearest again has-come for-us
Radiant, total happiness, my dearest, has come again for us.

Долго томилася, полно страдания, Сердце твоё, но поверь:
[dólga tam̡ilasa pólna stradán̡ija s̡értcɛ tvajó no pav̡ér̡]
long languished full of-suffering heart your but believe
Filled with suffering, your heart languished long; but believe me:

Дни одиночества, дни испытания Мы наверстаем теперь.
[d̡n̡í ad̡inóc̡ɛstva d̡n̡í ispytán̡ija mý nav̡ɛrstájɛm t̡ep̡ér̡]
days of-loneliness days of-trial we will-make-up-for now
Now we will make up for those days of loneliness and trial.

Нежные речи, любви выражения Вновь потекут без конца,
[n̡éžnyje‿r̡éc̡i l̡ubv̡í vyražén̡ija vnóf̡ pat̡ɛkúd‿b̡ɛskancá]
tender speeches of-love expressions again will-flow-forth without-end
Tender utterances, expressions of love again will flow forth, unrestrained.

И во единое снова биение Наши сольются сердца!
[i vajed̡inajɛ snóva b̡ijén̡ijɛ nášy sal̡jútca s̡ɛrtcá]
and into-single again beating our will-fuse hearts
And our hearts will merge anew into a single beating.

Пусть сочетает созвучье единое Наши две души, и вновь,
[pús̡t̡ sac̡ɛtájɛt sazvúc̡je‿jed̡ínajɛ nášy d̡v̡é dúšy i vnóf̡]
let combine accord single our two souls and again
Let a single accord unite our two souls, and again,

Словно весенняя песнь соловьиная, Наша воспрянет любовь.
[slóvna v̡es̡én̡n̡aja p̡és̡n̡ salav̡jínaja náša vas̡p̡rán̡ɛt l̡ubóf̡]
just-like spring song of-nightingale our will-awaken love
Like the nightingale's song of spring, our love will burst forth.

89. Уж гасли в комнатах огни... Соч. 63, № 5
'All the lights indoors had already gone out...'
(K.R.) (1887)

Уж гасли в комнатах огни... Благоухали розы...
[už‿gáşļi fkómnatax agņí blagauxáļi rózy]
already had-gone-out in-rooms lights gave-off-fragrance roses
All the lights indoors had already gone out. The air smelled of roses.

Мы сели на скамью в тени Развесистой берёзы.
[my şéļi naskaṃjú fţeņí raz̧ v̧éşistəj ḅeŗózy]
we sat-down on-bench in-shade of-spreading birch
We sat down on a bench in the shade of a spreading birch.

Мы были молоды с тобой. Так счастливы мы были
[my býļi mólady stabój tak şşáşļivy my býļi]
we were young with-you so happy we were
You and I were so young, we were so happy

Нас окружавшею весной, Так горячо любили!
[nás akružáfšeju v̧ɛsnój tág‿gaŗaçó ļuḅíļi]
us surrounding spring-time so ardently [we] loved
In that all-encompassing springtime, how ardently we loved.

Двурогий месяц наводил На нас своё сиянье;
[dvurógəj ṃéşac navaḑíl nanás svajó şijáņjɛ]
two-horned moon directed onto-us its glow
The crescent moon cast its glow on us.

Я ничего не говорил, Боясь прервать молчанье...
[ja ņiçɛvo ņɛgavaŗíl bajáş pŗɛrváţ malçáņjɛ]
I nothing did-not-say fearing to-break silence
I said nothing, fearing to break the silence.

Безмолвно синих глаз твоих Ты опускала взоры--
[ḅɛzmólvna şíņiɣ‿glás tvaíx ty apuskála vzóry]
wordlessly of-blue eyes your you lowered gaze
Without a word you would lower your deep-blue eyes...

Красноречивей слов иных   Немые разговоры.
[krasnaŗeçíyej slóf‿ynýx   ŋemýjɛ razgavóry]
more-eloquent   than-words other   mute   conversations
More eloquent than any words were your mute conversations.

Чему не смел поверить я,   Что в сердце ты таила,--
[çɛmú ŋeşmɛ́l   payéŗiţ já što fşértcɛ tý taíla]
what   did-not-dare   to-believe I   what in-heart   you concealed
All that I dared not believe, all that you withheld in your heart--

Всё это песня соловья   За нас договорила.
[fşó éta ŗéşŋa salayjá   zanás dagavaŗíla]
all   this song   of-nightingale   for-us   finished-saying
All this the nightingale expressed for us in its song.

90. Серенада (для тенора) Соч. 63, № 6
'Serenade (for tenor)'
(K.R.) (1887)

О дитя, под окошком твоим   Я тебе пропою серенаду…
[o ḑiţá padakóškam tvaím ja ţeƀé prapajú şeŗɛnádu]
oh child   under-window   your   I   to-you will-sing   serenade
Oh, my child, under your window I will sing you a serenade.

Убаюкана пеньем моим,   Ты найдёшь в сновиденьях отраду;
[ubajúkana ŗéŋjɛm maím ty najḑóš fsnayiḑéŋjax atrádu]
lulled   by-singing my   you   will-find in-dreams   joy
Lulled by my singing, you will find joy in your dreams.

Пусть твой сон и покой   В час безмолвный ночной
[púşţ⁻ tvój són‿y   pakój fçáz‿ƀɛzmólvnyj   naçnój]
let   your   sleep   and   repose   at-hour silent   nocturnal
May your dreams and repose at that silent hour of the night

Нежных звуков лелеют лобзанья!   Много горестей, много невзгод
[ŋéžnyɣ‿zvúkaf ļeļéjut labzáŋja mnóga góŗeşţej   mnóga ŋɛvzgót]
of-tender   sounds   foster   kisses   many   misfortunes many   adversities
Bring the kisses of soothing sounds. Many misfortunes, many adversities

Тебя в жизни, дитя, ожидает; Спи же сладко, пока нет забот,
[ţeḇá vžýẓņ ḑiţá ažydájɛt ṣp̦í žɛ slátka paká ņéd‿zabót]
you in-life child await sleep # sweetly while there-are-no cares
Await you in your life, my child. Sleep sweetly while there are still no cares,

Пока сердце тревоги не знает, Спи во мраке ночном
[paká ṣértcɛ ţŗɛvóg̦i ņɛznájɛt ṣp̦í vamrák̦ɛ nač̦nóm]
while heart alarm does-not-know sleep in-gloom of-night
While your heart is spared all alarm. Sleep in the gloom of night

Безмятежным ты сном, Спи, не зная земного страданья.
[ḇɛzm̦aţéžnym ty snóm ṣp̦í ņɛznája ẓɛmnóva stradáņja]
serene you sleep sleep not-knowing earthly suffering
Lost in serene dreams. Sleep, and know no earthly suffering

Пусть твой ангел-хранитель святой, Милый друг, над тобою летает
[púṣţ‾ tvój áng̦ɛl xraņíţeļ ṣṿatój m̦ílyj drúk nattabóju ļɛtájɛt]
let your angel guardian holy dear friend over-you fly
May your holy guardian angel fly over you, dearest friend,

И, лелея сон девственный твой, Тебе райскую песнь напевает,
[i ļeļéja són ḑéfṣţṿɛnnyj tvój ţeḇé rájskuju p̦éṣņ nap̦ɛvájɛt]
and cherishing dreams virginal your to-you heavenly song sing
And sing you a song of heaven, cherishing your innocent dreams.

Пу́сть той песни святой Отголосок живой
[púṣţ‾ tój p̦éṣņi ṣṿatój adgalósag‿žyvój]
let of-that song holy echo living
May the living echo of that holy song

Тебе в душу вселит упованье. Спи же, милая, спи, почивай
[ţeḇé vdúšu f̦ṣeļít upaváņjɛ ṣp̦í že‿m̦ílaja ṣp̦í pač̦iváj]
to-you in-soul inspire hope sleep # darling sleep repose
Instill hope in your soul. Sleep then, my darling, sleep, rest

Под аккорды моей серенады! Пусть приснится тебе светлый рай,
[padakórdy majéj ṣeŗɛnád púṣţ p̦ŗiṣņítca ţeḇé‿ṣṿétlyj ráj]
to-chords of-my serenade let appear-in-dream to-you bright paradise
To the chords of my serenade! May you dream of a bright paradise

Преисполненный вечно отрады; Пусть твой сон и покой
[p̧r̦eispólņennyj v̦éç̌na atrády púş̧t⁻tvój són‿y pakój]
overfilled eternally with-joy let your sleep and repose
Brimming over with happiness forever. May your dreams and repose

В час безмолвный ночной Нежных звуков лелеют лобзанья!
[fç̌áz‿b̦ezmólvnyj naç̌nój ņéžnyɣ‿zvúkaf ļeļéjut labzáņja]
at-hour silent nocturnal some-tender sounds foster of-kissing
At that silent hour of the night bring the kisses of soothing sounds.

91. Серенада 'Sérénade' Соч. 65, № 1
(E. Turquety, translated by A. Gorchakova) (1888)

Ты куда летишь, как птица, Юный сын младой денницы,
[ty kudá ļeţíš kak p̧ţica júnyj sýn mladój d̦eņņícy]
you where-to fly like bird young son of-new day
Where are you flying off to like a bird, young son of a brand new day,

Свежий, чистый ветерок, ветерок? Вдаль спешишь, того не зная,
[ş̧v̦éžyj ç̌istyj v̦eţerók v̦eţerók vdáļ şp̦ešýš tavó ņeznája]
fresh clean breeze breeze away [you] rush that not-knowing
Fresh, clean breeze? Away you rush, unaware

Что от страсти замирая, Каждый здесь дрожит листок!
[što atstráş̧ţi zam̦irája káždyj z̧d̦éz̧‿dražýt ļistók]
that from-passion expiring every here trembles leaf
That every leaf here is atremble, expiring from passion!

Иль в долину хочешь мчаться, В тёмных ивах покачаться,
[iļ vdaļínu xóç̌eš mç̌átca fţómnyx‿ývax pakaç̌átca]
or to-vale [you] want to-hasten in-dark willows to-rock
Or are you off to the vale, to rustle in the dark willows,

Где спит сладко соловей, спит меж ветвей? Хочешь к розе ты спуститься,
[gd̦é‿şp̦it slátka salav̦éj şp̦it m̦ežv̦eţv̦éj xóç̌eš króz̦e ty spuş̧ţítca]
where sleeps sweetly nightingale sleeps among-branches want onto-rose you to-settle
Where the nightingale sleeps sweetly amidst the branches? Do you want to alight on the rose,

С мотыльком ли порезвиться, В майский день, под блеском лучей?
[smatyļkóm ļi paŗez̧v̧ítca vmájskəj ḑéņ padb̧ļέskam luç̌éj]
with-butterfly # to-frolic on-May day under-glow of-rays
To frolic a bit with a butterfly, on this day in May, beneath the glow of rays?

Нет, лети зарёю ясной К той, кого люблю я страстно,
[ņέt ļeţí zaŗóju jásnəj któj kavó ļub̧ļú ja strásna]
no fly like-dawn bright to-her whom love I passionately
No! Fly like the bright dawn to the one I love passionately.

К ложу её понеси Запах роз и трав душистых,
[klóžu jejó paņeşí zápax rós‿y tráv‿dušýstyx]
to-couch her bear scent of-roses and grasses fragrant
Bear off to her couch the scent of roses and fragrant grasses,

Поцелуй мой нежный, чистый, Как дуновенье весны.
[pacεlúj moj ņέžnyj ç̌ístyj kag‿dunav̧éņje‿v̧εsný]
kiss my tender pure like breath of-spring
My kiss tender and pure, like a breath of spring!

92. Разочарование 'Déception' Соч. 65, № 2
(P. Collin, translated by A. Gorchakova) (1888)

Ярко солнце ещё блистало, Увидать хотел я леса,
[járka sónce‿jeş̧şó b̧ļistála uv̧idáţ xaţέl ja ļεsá]
brightly sun still shone to-see wanted I woods
The sun was still shining brightly. I decided I wanted to take a look at the woods

Где с весною вместе любви И блаженства пора настала
[gḑέ sv̧εsnóju v̧m̧éşţe‿ļubv̧í i blažέnstva pará nastála]
where with-spring together of-love and bliss time arrived
Where, together with spring, a time of love and bliss came for me

Подумал я: «В лесной тиши Её найду опять, как прежде,
[padúmal já vļεsnój ţišý jejó najdú ap̧áţ kak p̧ŗέžḑε]
thought I in-forest's stillness her [I] will-find again as formerly
I thought: "In the stillness of the forest I will find her again, as before.

И руки подав мне свои, Пойдёт за мной, полна надежды».
[i rúķi padáf mņɛ svaí pajḑód‿zamnój palná naḑéždy]
and hands having-given to-me her [she] will-follow me full of-hope
And giving me her hand, she will follow me, filled with expectation."

Я напрасно ищу... Увы! Взываю! Лишь эхо мне отвечает!
[ja naprásna iş̧şú uvý vzyváju ļiš éxo mņé atvyeçájɛt]
I in-vain seek alas [I] call-out only echo me answers
I seek her in vain. Alas! I call her name. Only an echo answers.

О, как скуден стал солнца свет! Как печален лес и безгласен!
[o kak skúḑɛn stál sónca şvét kak peçáļɛn ļés‿y ḅɛzgláşɛn]
oh how meager has-become of-sun light how sad forest and mute
Oh, how faint the sunlight has become! How sad and mute the forest!

О, любовь моя, как ужасно Так скоро утратить тебя!
[o ļubóf majá kak užásna tak skóra utráţiţ ţeḅá]
oh love my how awful so soon to-lose you
Oh, my love! How horrible to have lost you so soon!

93. Серенада 'Sérénade' Соч. 65, № 3
(P. Collin, translation by A. Gorchakova) (1888)

В ярком свете зари, блистающем и ясном, отблеск вижу дивных очей!
[vjárkam şvéţɛ zaŗí ḅļistájuş̧şɛm‿y jásnam ódḅļɛsk vížu ḑívnyx aç̧éj]
in-bright light of-dawn shining and clear reflection [I] see of-divine eyes
In the dawn's bright light, shining and clear, I see the reflection of your divine eyes!

Мнится, будто звучит в пеньи птиц сладкогласных
[mņítca bútta zvuç̧ít fpéņji ptíc slatkaglásnyx]
it-seems as-if sounds in-singing of-birds sweet-voiced
It seems I hear in the birds' sweet singing

Лишь эхо твоих детских речей!
[ļiš éxo tvaíɣ‿ḑétşķix ŗeç̧éj]
only echo of-your hild-like speeches
Only an echo of your child-like utterances.

В лилии нахожу твой покой безмятежный, твою чистоту в ней люблю!
[vļíļii naxažú tvoj pakój ḅɛzmaţéžnyj tvajú ç̧istatú vņéj ļuḅļú]
in-lily [I] find your peace serene your purity in-it [I] love
It is your serene calm that I find in the lily, your purity that I adore in it!

Запах роз, как твоё дыханье, сладко нежен,
[zápax rós kak tvajó dyxáŋjɛ slátka ŋɛ́žɛn]
scent of-roses like your breath [is] sweetly tender
The scent of roses, like your breath, is sweetly tender;

В розах я люблю свежесть твою.
[vrózax ja ļuḅļú ṣṿéžeṣṭ tvajú]
in-roses I love freshness your
It is your sweetness that I love in the rose!

И люблю я в волне в час бурный её прилива горячность и вспышки твои,
[i ļuḅļú ja vvalŋ́ɛ fc̦áz‿búrnyj jejó p̦ŗiļíva gaŗáč̦naṣṭ i fspýšķi tvaí]
and love I in-wave at-hour stormy of-its ebb impulsiveness and outbursts your
And in the stormy waves of ebb-tide I love your impulsiveness and outbursts,

Люблю я твои вопли и горя порывы в свисте ветра, в шуме грозы.
[ļuḅļú ja tvaí vóp̦ļi i góŗa parývy fṣṿíṣṭe‿ṿétra fšúm̦ɛ grazý]
love I your cries and of-woe fits in-whistling of-wind in-noise of-storm
It is your cries and fits of unhappiness that I love in the whistle of wind, in the noise of the storm.

Страсти пылкой твоей я люблю проявленье, жжёт она, точно солнца луч;
[stráṣṭi pýlkəj tvajéj ja ļuḅļú prajaṿļéŋjɛ ẑẑót aná tóč̦na sónca lúč̦]
of-passion fervent your I love manifestation burns it just-like of-sun ray
I love all manifestations of your fervent passion, which burns like the rays of the sun.

Луна в своей красе стыдливой -- твоё воплощенье,
[luná fsvajéj kraṣɛ́ styd̦ļívəj tvajó vaplaṣ̌ṣ̌éŋjɛ]
moon in-its beauty shy [is] your incarnation
The moon in its shy beauty is your incarnation,

Когда блестит нам из-за туч.
[kagdá ḅļeṣṭít nám izzatúč̦]
when [it] shines on-us from-behind-clouds
When it shines down on us through the clouds.

В юной, светлой весне я люблю возрожденье грёз чистых и надежд твоих;
[vjúnəj ṣṿétləj ṿeṣné‿ja ļuḅļú vazraž̦d̦éŋje‿gŗóṣ̌‿č̦ístyx‿y nad̦éšt¯ tvaíx]
in-young bright spring I love renascence of-dreams pure and hopes your
In the fresh young springtime I love the renascence of your pure dreams and hopes.

Люблю я твою печаль и страсть уединенья в тихом мраке теней ночных.
[ḷuḅḷú ja tvajú p̦eç̌áḷ i strás̹ţ ujeḓiņéņja fţixam mrák̦ɛ ţeņéj naç̌nýx]
love I your sadness and passion for-solitude in-quiet gloom of-shades nocturnal
I love your melancholy and passion for solitude in the quiet darkness of the night's shadows.

94. Пускай зима... 'Qu'importe que l'hiver...' Соч. 65, № 4
(P. Collin, translated by A. Gorchakova) (1888)

Пускай зима погасит солнца свелтый луч
[puskáj z̧imá pagás̹it sónca s̹v̹ɛ́tlyj lúç̌]
let winter extinguish of-sun bright ray
Let the winter extinguish the sun's bright rays

И покроет эфир цепью сумрачных туч...
[i pakrójɛt ef̦ír cép̦ju súmraç̌nyx túç̌]
and cover air with-chain of-dark clouds
And cover the skies with a chain of dark clouds...

Знаю я, где искать блеск света, солнца и лучей,
[znáju ja gḓe‿iskáḓ‿ḅḷésk s̹v̹ɛ́ta sónca i luç̌éj]
know I where to-look-for glow of-light of-sun and of-rays
I know where to look for the glow of light, of the sun's rays,

И рассвета, прекрасней зари в небесах.
[i rass̹v̹ɛ́ta p̦r̦ɛkrás̹ņej zaŗí vņeḅɛsáx]
and of-dawn lovelier than-sunrise in-heavens
Of the dawn, lovelier than a sunrise in the sky.

О, дорогая, в твоих лишь глазах!
[o daragája ftvaíx ḷiž‿glazáx]
oh darling in-your only eyes
Oh, my darling, in your eyes alone!

Пускай зима покроет снегом все цветы
[puskáj z̧imá pakrójɛt s̹ņégam f̦s̹ɛ́ cv̹ɛtý]
let winter cover with-snow all flowers
Let the winter cover all the flowers with snow

И суровой рукой рассеет лепестки...
[i suróvəj rukój rasşéjɛt ļeṗeşķi]
and with-stern hand scatter petals
And scatter all their petals with its stern hand...

Знаю я, где искать цвет прекрасный,
[znáju ja gḑe‿iskát̡ cɣét p̡r̡ɛkrásnyj]
know I where to-seek color lovely
I know where to look for lovely color,

Несмотря на холод дней ненастных,--
[ņɛsmaţŗá naxólad‿dņéj ņɛnásnyx]
in-spite of-coldness of-days inclement
Despite the coldness of season's foul weather--

Розу в свежей, пышной красе.
[rózu fşɣéžej pýšnəj kraşé]
rose in-fresh lush beauty
A rose in all its fresh, lush beauty.

О, дорогая,-- в твоей лишь душе!
[o daragája ftvajéj ļiž‿dušé]
oh darling in-your only soul
Oh, my darling, only in your soul!

Этот луч, что в глазах твоих всегда блестит,
[état lúç što vglazáx tvaíx fşɛgdá ḅļeşţít]
this ray that in-eyes your always shines
This gleam that is always shining in your eyes,

Которого ничто не может погасить;
[katórava ņištó ņɛmóžɛt pagaşíţ]
which nothing cannot extinguish
Which nothing can extinguish;

Тот цветок, что душа сохраняет,
[tót cɣɛtók što dušá saxraņájɛt]
that flower which soul preserves
That flower which your soul preserves,

Что никогда не увядает,
[što n̡ikagdá n̡euv̡adájɛt]
which never does-not-fade
Which never fades,

Пережив весенние дни.
[p̡er̡ɛžýf v̡es̡én̡n̡ije‿d̡n̡í]
having-survived spring days
Having lasted through all the days of spring.

О, дорогая, то блеск красы!
[o daragája to b̡l̡ɛ́sk krasý]
oh darling it-is glow of-beauty
Oh, my darling, it is the glow of your beauty.

95. Слёзы 'Les larmes' Соч. 65, № 5
(A. Blanchecotte, translated by A. Gorchakova) (1888)

Если покой дадите за все треволненья
[jés̡l̡i pakój dad̡ít̡ɛ zaf̡s̡é‿t̡r̡ɛvaln̡én̡ja]
if peace [you] will-give for-all troubles
If you can bring me solace for all my troubles

И смоете теперь дней минувших тоску,
[i smójet̡e‿t̡ep̡ér̡ d̡n̡éj m̡inúfšyx taskú]
and will-wash-off now of-days past grief
And can wash away all the grief of bygone years;

Если ранам всем моим несёте облегченье,
[jés̡l̡i ránam f̡s̡ɛ́m maím n̡es̡ót̡ɛ abl̡ex̡č̡én̡jɛ]
if to-wounds all my [you] bear relief
If you can bring healing to all my wounds,

Лейтесь, слёзы, я вас молю!
[l̡éjt̡es̡ s̡l̡ózy ja vás mal̡ú]
pour-forth tears I you implore
Pour forth, oh tears, I pray you!

Но, если и теперь вы смерть с собой несёте,
[no jéşļi i ţepéŗ vy şmţéŗţ ssabój ņeşóţɛ]
but if even now you death with-you bear
But if even now you are bringing death with you,

Если вы разжигать пламя сердца должны,
[jéşļi vy ražžygáţ pláma şértca dalžný]
if you to-kindle flame of-heart must
If you must kindle a flame in my heart,

Не мучьте же меня, зачем всю грудь мне рвёте?
[ņɛmúçţɛ že‿meņá zaçém fşú grúţ mņɛ rvóţɛ]
do-not-torment # me why whole breast to-me [you] tear
Do not torment me. Why do you tear at my heart?

О, слёзы, скройтесь вы! Да, скройтесь вы!
[o şļózy skrójţeş vy da skrójţeş vy]
oh tears hide-self you yes hide-self you
Oh tears, hide yourselves, hide yourselves!

Моя тоска ещё ужасней: пробудили вы вновь
[majá taská jeşşó užáşņej prabuḑíļi vy vnóf]
my grief [is] still more-terrible have-awakened you anew
My grief is made even greater: you have awakened anew

Горе прошлых годов!
[góŗɛ próšlyɣ‿gadóf]
pain of-past years
The pain of years gone by!

О, сжальтесь ещё и дайте смерть моей душе несчастной!
[o žžáļţeş jeşşó i dájţe‿şmţéŗţ majéj dušé ņeşşásnəj]
oh have-pity still and give death to-my soul miserable
Oh, have pity and grant death to my miserable soul!

Слёзы, застыньте вновь, да, застыньте вновь!
[şļózy zastýņţɛ vnóf da zastýņţɛ vnof]
tears congeal again yes congeal again
Tears, cease flowing once more, yes, cease flowing!

96. Чаровница 'Rondel' Соч. 65, № 6
(P. Collin, translated by A. Gorchakova) (1888)

Ты собою воплощаешь силу чар и волшебства:
[ty sabóju vaplaşşájɛš şílu çár‿y valšɛpstvá]
you in-self embody power of-charms and of-magic
You embody the power of charms and magic:

Радость, счастье и тоска от тебя придут, ты знаешь,
[rádaşş‿şşáştje‿i taská atţeþá pŗidút ty znájɛš]
joy happiness and grief from-you will-come you know
Joy and happiness, but also grief, will come from you, you know;

Но всем тем, кого пленяешь,
[no fşém ţém kavó pļeņájɛš]
but to-all those whom [you] captivate
But for all those who are in your power,

Рабства цепь не тяжела.
[rápstva cép ņeţažɛlá]
of-enslavement chain [is] not-heavy
Slavery's chain is not heavy.

Ты собою воплощаешь силу чар и волшебства!
[ty sabóju vaplaşşájɛš şílu çár‿y valšɛpstvá]
you in-self embody power of-charms and of-magic
You embody the power of charms and magic:

Да, победа не трудна:
[da paþéda ņɛtrudná]
yes victory [is] not-difficult
Yes, the victory is easy:

Взглядом, что ты нам бросаешь,
[vzgļádam što ty nám brasájɛš]
with-glance that you to-us throw
With the glance that you cast our way

Ты, как сетью, обнимаешь и ловишь у всех сердца...
[tý kak şéţju abņimájɛš‿y lóvìš ufşéx şɛrtcá]
you as with-net encompass and catch by-all hearts
You, as if with a net, encircle and capture all our hearts.

97. Мы сидели с тобой... 'We sat together...' Соч. 73, № 1
(D. Ratgauz) (1893)

Мы сидели с тобой у заснувшей реки.
[my şiḑéļi stabój uznasnúfšej ŗeķí]
we sat with-you by-sleeping river
We sat together beside the sleepy river.

С тихой песней проплыли домой рыбаки.
[sţíxəj ṗéşņej praplýļi damój rybaķí]
with-quiet song sailed-past going-home fishermen
Singing softly, fishermen heading home sailed past.

Солнца луч золотой за рекой догорал...
[sónca lúḑž‿zalatój zaŗεkój dagarál]
of-sun ray golden beyond-river subsided
Across the river the sunlight was subsiding...

И тебе я тогда ничего не сказал...
[i ţeḅé‿ja tagdá ņiçεvó ņεskazál]
and to-you I then nothing did-not-say
At that time I said nothing to you...

Загремело вдали... надвигалась гроза...
[zagŗeṃέla vdaļí naḑvigálaz‿grazá]
thundered in-distance was-brewing storm
There was thunder far off... a storm was coming up...

По ресницам твоим покатилась слеза...
[paŗeşņícam tvaím pakaţílaş şļezá]
along-lashes your rolled tear
A tear escaped your eyelashes...

И с безумным рыданьем к тебе я припал...
[i zḅεzúmnym rydáņjεm kţeḅέ ja ṗripál]
and with-mad sobs to-you I fell-down
And I fell at your feet, sobbing mindlessly...

И тебе ничего, ничего не сказал.
[i ţeḅé‿ņiçεvó ņiçεvó ņεskazál]
and to-you nothing nothing did-not-say
And I said nothing to you, nothing.

И теперь, в эти дни я, как прежде, один,
[i ţeper véţi dņí ja kak pŗéžde adín]
and now in-these days I as before [am] alone
And now, at present, as formerly, I am alone.

Уж не жду ничего от грядущих годин...
[uš ņeždú ņiçevó adgŗadúşşiɣ‿gadín]
already [I] do-not-expect nothing from-forthcoming years
I no longer anticipate anything from the years that lie ahead...

В сердце жизненный звук уж давно отзвучал
[fşértcɛ žýzņennyj zvúk už‿davnó adzvuçál]
in-heart of-life sound already long-since ceased-to-sound
The sound of life in my heart has long since ceased to be heard.

Ах, зачем я тебе ничего не сказал!...
[aɣ‿zaçém ja ţeþé ņiçevó ņeskazál]
ah why I to-you nothing did-not-say
Ah, why did I say nothing to you!

98. Ночь 'Night' Соч. 73, № 2
(D. Ratgauz) (1893)

Меркнет слабый свет свечи... Бродит мрак унылый...
[mérkņet slábyj şvét şveçí bródit mrák unýləj]
grows-dim weak light of-candle roams gloom melancholy
The candle's feeble light is fading... A melancholy gloom walks abroad...

И тоска сжимает грудь с непонятной силой...
[i taská žžymájed‿grúţ sņepaņátnəj şíləj]
and grief compresses breast with-incomprehensible force
And grief grips my heart with unfathomable force...

На печальные глаза тихо сон нисходит...
[napeçáļnyjɛ glazá ţixa són ņisxódit]
onto-sad eyes quietly sleep descends
Sleep quietly descends onto my sad eyes...

И с прошедшим в этот миг речь душа заводит.
[i sprašɛ́tšym vɛ́tat mi̦k ŗɛ́d̦ž̦‿dušá zavód̦it]
and with-past at-this instant speech soul strikes-up
And at this instant my soul strikes up a conversation with the past.

Истомилася она горестью глубокой.
[istami̦lasa aná góŗeşţju glubókəj]
has-grown-weary it from-sorrow deep
It has grown weary from deep sorrow.

Появись же, хоть во сне, о мой друг далёкий!...
[pajav̦íž‿žɛ xoţ vaşņɛ́ o moj drúg‿daļókəj]
appear # at-least in-dreams oh my friend distant
Appear to me, my dear, far-off friend, at least in my dreams.

99. В эту лунную ночь... 'On this moon-lit night...' Соч. 73, № 3
(D. Ratgauz) (1893)

В эту лунную ночь, в эту дивную ночь,
[vɛ́tu lúnnuju nóç̦ vɛ́tu d̦ívnuju nóç̦]
on-this moon-lit night on-this wondrous night
On this moon-lit night, on this glorious night,

В этот миг благодатный свиданья,
[vɛ́tat mi̦g‿blagadátnyj şv̦idáņja]
at-this moment blessed of-meeting
At this heavenly moment of meeting,

О, мой друг, я не в силах любовь превозмочь,
[o moj drúk ja ņɛ fşílax ļubóf̦ p̦ŗɛvazmóç̦]
oh my friend I [am] not able love to-surmount
Oh, my friend, I can resist my love no longer,

Удержать я не в силах признанья!
[ud̦ɛržáţ ja ņɛ fşílax p̦ŗiznáņja]
to-restrain I [am] not able admission
I cannot hold back my declaration!

В серебре чуть колышется озера гладь…
[fșeŗeḅŗé‿çuț kalýšɛtsa óẓɛra gláț]
in-silver barely flutters of-lake smooth-surface
The lake's smooth surface ripples ever so slightly in the silvery light…

Наклонясь, зашепталися ивы…
[naklaņáẓ‿zašɛptáļisa ívy]
bending-low have-begun-to-whisper willows
Bending low, the willows are whispering together…

Но бессильны слова! Как тебе передать
[no ḅɛșșíļny slavá kak țeḅé‿ṗeŗɛdáț]
but [are] powerless words how to-you to-convey
But words are useless! How am I to convey to you

Истомлённого сердца порывы?
[istaṃļónnava șértca parývy]
of-exhausted heart outbursts
The outbursts of an anguished heart?

Ночь не ждёт, ночь летит…
[nóç ņɛžḑót nóç ļețít]
night does-not-wait night flies
The night waits for no one, it flies on…

Закатилась луна… Заалело в таинственной дали…
[zakațílaș luná zaaļéla ftaínșțṿɛnnəj dáļi]
has-set moon it-has-grown-scarlet in-mysterious distance
The moon has set; the sky glows scarlet in the magical distance…

Дорогая, прости! Снова жизни волна
[daragája prașțí snóva žýẓņi valná]
beloved farewell again of-life wave
Farewell, beloved! Once again the wave of life

Нам несёт день тоски и печали!
[nám ņeșód‿ḑéņ taşķí i ṗeçáļi]
to-us bears day of-grief and sadness
Brings us another day of grief and sadness.

100. Закатилось солнце... 'The sun has set...' Соч. 73, № 4
(D. Ratgauz) (1893)

Закатилось солнце, заиграли краски Лёгкой позолотой в синеве небес...
[zakaţilaş sóncɛ zaigráļi kráşķi ļóxkəj pazalótəj fşiņeyé‿ņeḅés]
has-set sun have-started-to-play colors of-light gilding in-blue of-heavens
The sun has set, a faint golden hue has begun to glisten in the deep blue of the heavens...

В обаяньи ночи сладострастной ласки Тихо что-то шепчет задремавший лес...
[vabajáņji nóçi sladastrásnəj láşķi ţíxa štóta šέpçɛt zaḑrɛmáfšyj ļέs]
in-charm of-night of-voluptuous caresses quietly something whispers dozing forest
The slumbering forest whispers something softly, lost in the voluptuous caresses of the night.

И в душе тревожной умолкают муки
[i vdušé‿ţŗɛvóžnəj umalkájut múķi]
and in-soul alarmed grow-silent torments
And all pain is assuaged in my troubled soul,

И дышать всей грудью в эту ночь легко...
[i dyšáţ fşéj grúḑju vέtu nóç ļɛxkó]
and to-breathe with-whole chest in-this night [is] easy
And on such a night deep, deep breathing is easy...

Ночи дивной тени, ночи дивной звуки
[nóçi ḑívnəj ţéņi nóçi ḑívnəj zvúķi]
of-night marvellous shadows of-night marvellous sounds
The shadows and sounds of the wondrous night

Нас с тобой уносят, друг мой, далеко
[nás stabój unóşad‿drúk moj daļɛkó]
us with-you bear-away friend my far
Transport us far, far away, my dearest.

Вся объята негой этой ночи страстной,
[fşá abjáta ņέgəj έtəj nóçi strásnəj]
all encompassed by-bliss of-this night passionate
Caught up in the bliss of this passionate night,

Ты ко мне склонилась на плечо главой...
[ty kamņέ sklaņílaş napļɛçó glavój]
you to-me leaned onto-shoulder head
You have leaned your head on my shoulder...

Я безумно счастлив, о, мой друг прекрасный,
[ja b̦ɛzúmnɑ ș̦ș̦áș̦l̦if o moj drúk p̦r̦ɛkrásnəj]
I [am] madly happy oh my friend lovely
I am insanely happy, my lovely darling,

Бесконечно счастлив в эту ночь с тобой!
[b̦ɛskan̦éç̦nɑ ș̦ș̦áș̦l̦if vέtu nóç̦ stabój]
boundlessly happy in-this night with-you
Boundlessly happy to share this night with you!

101. Средь мрачных дней... 'Amidst dreary days...' Соч. 73, № 5
(D. Ratgauz) (1893)

Средь мрачных дней, под гнётом бед, Из мглы туманной прошлых лет,
[ș̦r̦ɛd̦mráç̦nyɣ‿d̦n̦éj padgn̦ótam b̦έt izmglý tumánnəj próšlyx l̦έt]
amidst-dreary days under-pressure of-misfortunes out-of-gloom foggy of-past years
Amidst dreary days, under the weight of woes, out of the hazy gloom of years gone by,

Как отблеск радостных лучей Мне светит взор твоих очей.
[kak ódb̦l̦esk rádasnyx luç̦éj mn̦e‿ș̦v̦έțid‿vzór tvaíx aç̦éj]
like reflection of-joyous rays to-me shines gaze of-your eyes
Like a reflection of rays of joy, the radiant gaze of your eyes shines upon me.

Под обаяньем светлых слов Мне снится, я с тобою вновь.
[padabaján̦jɛm ș̦v̦έtlyx slóf mn̦e‿ș̦n̦ítcɑ ja stabóju vnóf̦]
under-spell of-cheery words to-me is-dreamed I with-you [am] again
Under the spell of your cheerful words, I dream that I am with you once more.

При свете дня, в ночной тиши Делюсь восторгами души.
[p̦r̦iș̦v̦έțe‿d̦n̦á vnɑç̦nój țišý d̦ɛl̦úș̦ vastórgam̦i dušý]
in-light of-day in-night's quiet [I] share raptures of-spirit
Whether in the light of day or the quiet of night, I share all spiritual joys with you.

Я вновь с тобой! Моя печаль Умчалась в пасмурную даль...
[ja vnóf̦ stabój majá p̦ɛç̦ál̦ umç̦álaș̦ fpásmurnuju dál̦]
I [am] again with-you my sadness has-vanished into-murky distance
I am with you again! My sadness has fled into the murky distance...

И страстно вновь хочу я жить-- Тобой дышать, тебя любить!
[i strásna vnóf̧ xaç̌ú ja žýţ tabój dyšáţ ţeb̧á ļub̧íţ]
and passionately again want I to-live you to-breathe you to-love
And ardently again I long to live--to live you, to breathe you, to love you.

102. Снова, как прежде, один... 'Again, as before, alone...' Соч. 73, № 6
(D. Ratgauz) (1893)

Снова, как прежде, один, Снова объят я тоской...
[snóva kak p̧ŗɛ́žḑɛ aḑín snóva abját ja taskój]
again as before alone again gripped [am] I by-grief
Again I am alone, as before. Again I am gripped by grief.

Смотрится тополь в окно, Весь озарённый луной.
[smóţŗitca tópaļ vaknó v̧éş azaŗónnyj lunój]
looks-at-self poplar in-window all illumined by-moon
A poplar looks in at my window, all aglow in the moonlight.

Смотрится тополь в окно... Шепчут о чём-то листы...
[smoţŗitca tópaļ vaknó šɛ́pç̌ut aç̌ómta ļistý]
looks-at-self poplar in-window whisper about-something leaves
A poplar looks in at my window... Its leaves whisper something...

В звёздах горят небеса... Где теперь, милая, ты?
[vz̧v̧ózdaɣ‿gaŗát ņeb̧ɛsá gḑé‿ţep̧éŗ m̧ílaja tý]
in-stars burn heavens where now darling [are] you
The sky is afire with stars... Where are you now, my beloved?

Всё, что творится со мной, Я передать не берусь...
[f̧şó što tvaŗítca samnój já p̧eŗɛdáţ ņeb̧ɛrúş]
all that is-happening with-me I to-convey will-not-undertake
I cannot begin to convey to you all that I am going through...

Друг! помолись за меня, Я за тебя уж молюсь!...
[drúk pamalíz̧‿zam̧eņá já zaţeb̧á už maļúş]
friend pray for-me I for-you already pray
Pray for me, my darling! I already pray for you!